WALKING HIS TRAIL
SIGNS OF GOD ALONG THE WAY

SIGNS OF
GOD ALONG
THE WAY

+

WALKING

REAL-LIFE STORIES FROM THE BESTSELLING AUTHOR OF *END OF THE SPEAR*

HIS TRAIL

+

STEVE SAINT
AND **GINNY SAINT**

SALT**RIVER**®

AN IMPRINT OF
Tyndale House Publishers, Inc.

Visit Tyndale's exciting Web site at www.tyndale.com

TYNDALE is a registered trademark of Tyndale House Publishers, Inc.

SaltRiver and the SaltRiver logo are registered trademarks of Tyndale House Publishers, Inc.

Walking His Trail: Signs of God along the Way

Designed by Erik M. Peterson

Library of Congress Cataloging-in-Publication Data

Saint, Steve.
    Walking His trail : signs of God along the way / Steve Saint.
      p. cm.
    Includes bibliographical references (p.   ).
    ISBN-13: 978-1-4143-1376-4 (sc)
    ISBN-10: 1-4143-1376-4 (sc)
    1. Saint, Steve. 2. Huao Indians—Missions. 3. Missionaries—Ecuador—Biography. 4. Missionaries—Violence against—Ecuador. 5. Huao Indians—Religion. 6. Huao Indians—Social life and customs. I. Saint, Ginny. II. Title.
    F3722.1.H83S343 2007
    266.0092′273—dc22
    [B]   2007017429

Printed in the United States of America

13 12 11 10 09 08 07
 7 6 5 4 3 2 1

The author has used a mixture of orthographies in spelling Waodani names and words in order to most accurately reflect Waodani pronunciations for English-speaking readers.

+

Ginny and I dedicate this little book to our parents
who started us walking His trail with their human
and fallible but believable example.

Steve

CONTENTS

AUTHOR'S NOTE

+

"Stevie-boy, your daddy is never going to get to come home and live with us again." Mom had called me into her bedroom to give me this terrible, mind-numbing information. My dad, Nate Saint, and four friends, Jim Elliot, Ed McCully, Pete Fleming, and Roger Youderian, had just been brutally speared to death by warriors from a Stone Age tribe they were trying to befriend and protect. I was only a little boy. My dad was my hero. And this news was devastating. But there were chapters to come in my life that were as wonderful as that early chapter was excruciating.

I now know all the members of the attack party that killed dad and his friends. I have lived with them. They have loved me and cared for me and my wife and children and grandchildren. The very same people who killed my family have become family to me.

God intervenes in people's lives all the time. But we seldom document these special, faith-building events. I think we should write them down so we will remember them and can pass them on. Why don't I go first?

INTRODUCTION: SAND CASTLES

+

"It takes faith to believe that the world as we see it today is the product of evolution, but there *is* some evidence on which to base that faith. For instance, X-rays of a seal's flippers show that each flipper has five longitudinal bones, very much like the bones in an ape or human hand. Now doesn't that make you wonder if they couldn't have ascended from the same ancestral origin? Why else would the bones in a seal's flipper resemble those in a primate's hand?"

The twenty or so teenagers in the room sat perfectly still. A dead silence permeated the room. Then on inspiration, someone blurted out, "Yes, but the similarity could just as likely show that both people and seals are created by the same Creator who used similar designs for both."

That was exactly the answer I was looking for. Unfortunately, it was my wife, Ginny, who came up with it. I wasn't sure that the teenagers had yet grasped the point I had been trying to make, which was that reasonable and educated people sit on both sides of the table when it comes to the question of God's existence and His role in the universe.

So I continued. "There is evidence that can be used to support the theory of evolution. There is also evidence that indicates that this world is the handiwork of an intelligent Creator. Both sides in this debate prefer to believe that the other side consists only of people who are incapable of intelligent thought."

Most of the young people in the group that Wednesday

night were from evangelical Christian backgrounds. They were a little surprised and uncomfortable when I mentioned that there is some evidence to support evolution. They were totally unprepared, however, for what happened next.

Pablo, our recently arrived exchange student from Spain, blurted out with obvious conviction in his voice and an intense expression on his face: "But there is no evidence for God."

It was clear that just as the majority of the group had been taught to think of evolution as an untenable theory, Pablo had been taught that there was no tangible evidence to suggest the existence of God.

After the meeting, Pablo was waiting to talk. It soon became apparent that although this highly intelligent young man had been led to believe that God's existence was simply the fabrication of human imagination, he was not totally opposed to the concept of God. He simply saw no confirming evidence.

As we debated the existence of God, I searched for a mutually agreeable starting point. I had once heard a story about a man who claimed he was dead. His family and friends tried to convince him that he was not dead, but he remained convinced he was. Finally a psychologist was called in to help. He questioned the deluded "dead" man until the two of them found a characteristic of dead people they both agreed upon. They agreed that dead people don't bleed. As soon as they had established this point, the psychologist produced a needle and pricked the patient. As a spot of blood began to grow on the man's arm, the psychologist asked, "Now what do you think about being dead?" The man answered, "Well, what do you know—dead people *do* bleed."

I was looking for a point of mutual agreement from which

to start a sincere conversation with Pablo. As we were debating, a picture came to mind of a recent trip we had taken with Pablo to Daytona Beach. While we were there, we had seen some very elaborate sand castles.

"Pablo, let's suppose you are stranded like Robinson Crusoe on a deserted island. Desperate for company, you search the small island repeatedly, looking for another human. Finally, after exhaustively searching the entire island, you resign yourself to the fact that you are totally and completely alone. Then one morning you walk down to the ocean, and there on the beach you find a finely detailed and elaborate sand castle. Now what would you believe? Would you prefer to believe that some rogue wave from the last receding tide created the castle, or would you decide that in spite of your belief to the contrary, there must be other intelligent life on the island?"

Pablo looked as though he felt trapped, but he didn't hesitate long. "I would have to believe that someone else was on the island," he responded. "Waves don't make sand castles; people do." Then with an intense expression that hinted at defiance but spoke clearly of a deep-seated yearning I have often felt myself, he demanded, "But where are *life's* sand castles? Where are the signs of God along the way?"

Pablo's demand is a fair one. God is only significant to us if He intervenes in our lives!

I set out to establish intellectual evidence of God's existence for Pablo. But Pablo did not respond to intellectual arguments. He wanted to hear that I had actually experienced God. He wanted me to show him the signs of God's personal intervention in my life and the lives of people I knew.

Over the course of the next few weeks, I had the opportunity to tell Pablo of some of the sand castles God has built along my life's shoreline. Before he left, Ginny and I took Pablo and our kids over to New Smyrna Beach for a few days. On our first night there, we all went for a walk along the nearly deserted beach. As we returned to our condominium, the sun was just a rosy glow in the western sky. We nearly walked over it before we saw it—but there on the beach was an intricately detailed sand structure: moat, tower, castle, and bridge. I glanced at Pablo just as he looked over at me.

Thanks to Pablo's challenge, I decided to document some of the signs of God's intervention in my life as I have been walking His trail. The tides of time have already erased many of them from my mind, but on the following pages you'll see that some remain strong and clear. I'm sharing them in the hope that they will encourage and stimulate you to recognize and document your own sand castles for those who come after you.

Your story is the greatest legacy you will leave to your friends. It's the longest-lasting inheritance you will leave to your heirs. So watch for signs of God's intervention in your life, and record those stories for your children, grandchildren, and great-grand-children as you walk God's trail.

Ginny and I hope that our story will motivate you to notice God's signs in your own life, and pass them on.

XIV

CHAPTER 1

OUT OF THE SKY

MIRACLE WIFE

SAND CASTLES

AUTHOR'S NOTE

The old bus was in bedlam as thirty-two young men and women tried to outshout everyone else. On one side of the road was a vertical wall of rock. On the other side, a sheer drop-off. Excitement and adventure were in the air as we careened around hairpin turns. The road was little more than a notch cut out of the mountainside as we wound our way out of the Andes Mountains to the jungles below.

But mingled with the excitement was also a little fear. Visions of snakes and monster spiders played just beneath the surface as each person sought reassurance from the others. I was the tour leader for this musical group and the only one with any jungle experience. It was up to me to either ease everyone's fears or fuel the fires of apprehension.

"What kinds of animals will we see?" someone yelled from the back. "Are there any camels?"

This was too good to pass up. "Sure," I yelled back.

1

"Amazonian camels, with webbed feet for swimming in jungle rivers and green spots for camouflage." The bus roared with laughter, and soon everyone began to ride the joke. Every question of "What's that?" was met with a chorus of "It's a camel!"

Our destination was Puyo, a little one-street frontier town on the edge of the jungle. Once there, we had just enough time to unpack the equipment and walk to the auditorium before the group was scheduled to perform a musical concert.

As we made our way down the dirt "main street," someone tried the gag one more time: "Hey, look, a camel!" Without thinking, I glanced over at the pasture where he was pointing. Evening shadows were playing tricks on us, and an old horse on the far end of the pasture *did* look almost like a camel.

Just as I was about to make a joke about being duped by an old nag standing in front of a giant anthill, the animal stood up. I had never seen a camel outside of a zoo, but I knew one when I saw it, and I was sure enough seeing one now.

"No camels, huh? What do you call that?" Everyone was kidding *me* now! I didn't know how that desert buggy ended up in the Amazon rain forest, but I knew I was going to take a lot of ribbing on this one—especially, I hoped, from Virginia, one of the older girls in the group whose beautiful eyes, dimples, and contagious enthusiasm had caught my attention.

When the concert was over, that crazy camel was lying down right in the middle of the plaza. I had never seen a camel up close, though I didn't admit it, so I was as eager as anyone for a closer look.

"Can we ride him?" Virginia asked. She was so pretty she made my knees weak.

"Sure," I replied. "Why not?" Without a second's hesitation, this Scandinavian siren was shinnying up the camel's back, formal dress and all.

I didn't know much about dromedarian character, but I knew those weren't happy sounds coming from the camel. I could just picture him biting one of those cute little feet hanging enticingly down his back, and I knew I would be responsible!

I can't remember how I got her down, but I do remember how erratically my heart beat when I did. Any girl this beautiful and adventuresome was sure to have a line of young men waiting back home in Minnesota. But even so, I began to wonder if maybe my resignation to bachelorhood at twenty-two had been a little premature.

I had resigned myself to being single when I graduated from Wheaton College and headed home to Ecuador. I had just broken my engagement with a young schoolteacher from Wisconsin. Our relationship had been somewhat stormy. She was a nice girl from a wonderful Christian home, so I figured the storm was mostly my doing. Who would ever want to marry an adventuresome but contemplative "jungle boy"? Girls wanted security and stability. Nice girls wanted to live in a small town within driving distance of a good hospital for delivering babies and a nice dinner theater for contemplating their children.

I loved mountain climbing and felt as comfortable living in the jungles as I did in suburbia. I was tricultural, bilingual, well traveled, and restless. I desperately wanted to get married, but I didn't think I'd make much of a husband unless I could design the bride. My order was pretty unrealistic, even for God. I wanted a girl who shared my desire to live life by "the Book." She would love to sit at home and read on a rainy day, but she wouldn't care where the rain was falling. She would make our home a castle whether it had four bedrooms under barrel tile or one room under thatch. She would feel comfortable mingling at a political rally or dishing out gruel in a disaster-relief kitchen. And she would look stunningly beautiful at either. It also wouldn't hurt if she liked to fly, scuba dive, mountain climb, and travel, all while raising a big family.

I was idealistic, but I was also realistic enough to know my chances of finding such a wife were about as good as finding a camel in the Amazon. The clincher was that I wanted to know that Miss Impossibly Wonderful would mean it if she said, "For better or worse, in sickness and in health, till death do us part." And I wanted to mean it too! With the national divorce rate reaching the 50 percent mark, I knew I was asking for another miracle there. *And oh, by the way, God, would You mind bringing her to Ecuador? I'll be working in an orphanage as a volunteer and starting a construction and land development business while I try to figure out what You want me to do with my life,* I had prayed.

After a brief trek into the jungles, we headed back up the winding road to the mountains, where I planned to leave the tour and return to my responsibilities at my construction business and at the orphanage where I volunteered. I knew I had to figure out some way to get to know Virginia before we were separated forever. I was desperate to figure out some excuse to get her away from the group so we could talk. That would have been difficult enough, but every time I was around her, I was unusually shy and unsure of myself.

It was a class B miracle that Virginia, a full-time nurse, had been able to join her old singing group for the tour. It was probably a class C divine intervention that *I* had been chosen as tour leader for their jungle trip. Now I needed—and received—a class A miracle.

We stopped in the city of Ambato to spend the night before continuing on to the capital city of Quito. I knew this would be my last chance to talk to Virginia, but I just couldn't figure out how to approach her. I was not only low on courage, but I also sorely lacked a good strategy. My desperate mind pulsated between trying to remember some boy-meets-beautiful-girl-and-wittily-impresses-her phrase, and begging God to intervene.

I got my miracle so fast that I later kicked myself for not asking for something more substantial than just the opportunity to talk. I heard my name, and there was Virginia—or "Ginny," as her friends called her—asking if I had a few minutes to talk to her after dinner.

It is a good thing my heart almost stopped and my knees and tongue froze momentarily. It would have been embarrassing and might even have scared Ginny if I had fallen to my knees to lavish God with praises for such an immediate answer to my prayer. Instead, my temporary paralysis gave an air of appropriate contemplation before answering that yes, I'd be glad to take a few minutes (not to exceed a week or so) if she wanted to talk.

It has never taken so long or given me less pleasure to eat a filet mignon. Hope is a wonderful inspiration, but when it causes a rush of adrenaline it dulls the sense of taste and makes chitchatting and sitting still difficult.

Finally it was just Virginia Lynn Olson and Stephen Saint in the hotel rose garden sharing tidbits of our pasts and discussing the challenges of life. Ginny was impressed, she said, that a young man would graduate from college to work in an orphanage and build houses for missionaries rather than taking a corporate job and buying an expensive car, especially since everyone else our age seemed to be doing just that. She was not flirting or being aggressive; she was simply looking for hope that there were still young men around who wanted God to have first priority in life, men who wanted the significance of their lives to be measured in more than the accumulation of toys or social status.

I told Ginny how forlorn I had felt returning to Ecuador, where I would be almost totally out of social circulation. I didn't feel that I was as great a specimen of principle, virtue, and spirituality as she seemed to perceive. But I did want God to be first in my life, and I did want my life to have eternal significance. I was also desperately lonely, and I wanted to get to know this lovely, beautiful, and sensitive young woman before she flew out of my life forever. As we talked, I realized that Ginny was naturally quite shy and unsure of herself around strangers. It really had been a miracle that she had found the courage to approach me. I figured that it was now up to me to initiate further contact.

I couldn't finagle an invitation to accompany the tour on their next outing to the coast of Ecuador because there wasn't room on the bus. I also couldn't leave my construction crews without supervision, so I resorted to writing. I wrote Ginny a letter, thirteen pages if I remember, telling her how wonderful it was to talk to her in Ambato. The knowledge that our time was running out made me bold, so I told her how alive I had felt just being around her for three days and how I missed her even though I didn't know her. I even hinted that maybe God had made our paths cross and that I would like the opportunity to take her out when her group returned from the coast.

What I didn't tell Ginny was the reason I was beginning to

see more than coincidence in our meeting. The night before I had joined them for their tour of the jungles, the "Bright Expectations" had performed a Sunday evening program in our English Fellowship Church in Quito.

At that concert, Mrs. Kelly, the woman who had organized the tour and asked me to accompany them to the jungles, sat down beside me. She began to tease me about what wonderful wives Scandinavian women made. Mrs. Kelly and her husband were missionaries of the Swedish Covenant Church, and it was obvious that the group had a large contingent with Scandinavian descent.

I would have just ignored Mrs. Kelly's remarks if it hadn't been for two things. The first was that Mrs. Kelly was usually reserved and quiet. It seemed terribly out of character for her to even sit by me, much less tease me. Second, she continued the teasing even after the program began. I knew our whispering was beginning to bother those around us, and I knew nobody would believe that it was Mrs. Kelly initiating it, so when she insisted that I choose one of the girls to marry, I did it just to put an end to the conversation. A girl with a sweet, soft voice was singing a solo right at that moment. I couldn't see who it was, but I told Mrs. Kelly I would marry the soloist.

The next morning when I showed up to join the group, Mrs. Kelly was waiting for me. She grabbed my arm and marched me up to one of the buses that was already loaded. "That's your girl," she said, pointing right at Virginia, "so you ride her bus." I thought she had just picked out the prettiest girl in the group and was teasing me again.

"How do you know she's the one I chose last night? We couldn't see her," I challenged.

"Oh, that's easy," she replied. "All the soloists are listed in the bulletin." With that she ushered me to the bus, where thankfully, Virginia was unaware that her nuptial arrangements with a total stranger had just been finalized. Mrs. Kelly never teased me again—about anything.

Ginny received my thirteen-page epistle when the group got back from the coast. She says now that she was excited to get it but felt it would be too forward to write back. Her initiative in Ambato had apparently been a wide deviation from her normally shy character. Fortunately, or providentially, Mrs. Kelly insisted that Ginny reply. She also insisted that Ginny do so immediately so that Mrs. Kelly could hand deliver it to my house on her way home.

I followed up Ginny's note with a telephone call and asked if I could take her to dinner and show her the lights of our beautiful city of Quito, nestled like a sparkling gem in a setting of snowcapped mountains.

Only after setting a time—and we had precious little time left—did I remember that I already had an inviolable engagement for the same evening: my stepbrother Joel's groom's dinner. I couldn't let my brother down; I was his best man. But I also couldn't pass up this only chance to be with Ginny. So, with several apologies and a suspiciously detailed assurance that I hadn't planned to introduce her to my whole family on our first date, I did just that.

My embarrassment quickly faded once we arrived at the party. Everyone seemed to accept Ginny and really like her from the start. I did too, so we said our good-byes and made a hasty exit.

I had long wondered what real romantic love felt like. I had looked for definitions and descriptions, but they were always a bit vague or imprecise, like receiving directions from people who have been to your destination many times. They can picture every turn and landmark, and they usually end with "you can't miss it!" But what they really mean is that *they* can't miss it. An older man had once told me that love comes in different packages for different people. "But," he said, "when you really find it, you'll know it." I wasn't so sure I would know. I wanted a checklist. I knew that it is possible to think you're in love but not be. But it wasn't until I met Ginny that I realized you can't be in love and think you're not.

I had it and I knew it. The world could have burned down around me and I would have been oblivious. You could have pulled my fingernails out and I would have merely overlooked it. What I couldn't overlook was that Ginny was leaving and I couldn't follow. I had sixty men working for me. I had commitments to fulfill that forced my body and mind to stay in Ecuador. But my heart flew back to Minnesota with Virginia Lynn Olson.

After a month or so of being apart, I knew I had to find a solution to the problem. It took about two seconds to figure out that the answer to my problem was living in the north-central part of the United States. It took somewhat longer to figure out how to keep sixty men busy for two weeks while I was away. I finally decided that this was the opportune time to build everyone in our little development a septic system or two if necessary. With that problem solved, I found out that I had another one. All flights out of Quito bound for Miami were sold out for the foreseeable future. Besides that, I had recently received Ecuadorean and U.S. dual citizenship, which meant that I needed military permission and a U.S. visa to leave the country. I got the military permission, but the U.S. Embassy refused to give me a U.S. visa because I held a U.S. passport.

Finally I bought a standby ticket, called Ginny by international telephone, and headed to the airport. The airport officials made a stink about my papers but eventually accepted them with the warning that the U.S. authorities would not accept my dual citizenship. But there was a bigger problem. The plane was sold out. In South America, who you know is very important. I happened to know someone who knew the man at the exit gate, and he let me board the plane to look for a seat. I found one and quickly settled in, trying to look inconspicuous. Just then, two women boarded the plane. I had taken the very last seat, which had unfortunately been sold to them. Fortunately it had been sold to both of them! They started fighting over that seat and put up such a ruckus that the pilot called security and had them both thrown off the plane. That left me as the happy occupier of that last seat.

Minnesota was never as beautiful as it was that summer of 1973. Crab apples were a little sweeter, butterflies a little more colorful, and the smell of newly mown hay just a bit more appealing than usual. Summer days are usually long in the North, but this summer they flew by. I had to return to Ecuador much sooner than I wanted to.

By this time, Ginny and I had spent a total of thirteen days together: three on the tour observing each other and ten in Minnesota getting to know each other. Neither of us thought we knew the other one well, but we knew the fundamentals. We both wanted to follow God's plan for our lives. I wanted a loyal friend to accompany me on the strenuous and uncertain journey of life. Ginny wanted a man she could trust to lead the way. It was clear that Ginny trusted me. I knew her devotion and trust would be powerful motivation to keep me on course.

Besides all that, there was magic between us. We were in love and we dreaded being separated again.

Since there was no one who could finish my work in Ecuador, I talked to Ginny about quitting her job and coming to serve as a volunteer nurse in Hospital Vos Andes, a mission hospital in Quito. I knew it was highly likely that we might live overseas if we were to marry, and I also knew it was important that Ginny realize what it was like to actually live in a third world country. Leaving the security of her hometown, family, friends, work, and church would also give Ginny a chance to separate love from infatuation.

Plenty of my college acquaintances had married before putting their love and commitment to the test. When the trials of life came, they found that they had insufficient love and commitment. I had watched them split up one after the other, and I had no interest in a false start. Nor did I wish to prove my tenacity by living in an unhappy and unhealthy relationship. I wanted the magic to last and last and to never wear out! So Ginny followed me to Ecuador.

Our testing started about the time Ginny cleared customs. She couldn't fend for herself in a foreign country with a strange culture and an unknown language, so my mom and stepdad invited Ginny to live with them. Mom and Dad loved her from the start, but I'm sure it was more than a little uncomfortable living under such close scrutiny while being so dependent on my parents.

Ginny's new job in Ecuador offered another test. Everyone liked this senorita with a quick smile and cute dimples. But the patients thought she was just a little girl. It is quite proper for young Latin girls to remain silent when spoken to by an adult. This is seen as respectful shyness. Ginny played the shy role very well, partly because she *was* shy and partly because she didn't speak Spanish. What she didn't understand was that when her patients finished talking, she was supposed to respectfully leave. Instead, she assumed that their silence was the signal that they were ready for their injections, which was usually what she had been sent to do.

"No, little girl," the patients often said, "don't give me the shot; call the nurse."

Adding to everything else, I was terribly busy. I generally worked ten to twelve hours a day, six days a week. By the time I got cleaned up and drove from the construction site back to the city, I didn't have much time or energy left. But Ginny never faltered. She was sweet as sugar with my parents and hard-working and understanding at the hospital. I was still helping out at the orphanage on the weekends, and the children there loved Ginny. So did I!

I wanted to marry Ginny, and she made it clear that she would say yes when I asked. But could we make such a permanent commitment? I couldn't help but think of all my friends whose marriages had failed after only a short time. Who gets married thinking it won't work? Who walks down the aisle planning to take that special person to court in three or four or twenty years? I had seen how easily fortunes could change, as well as perspectives.

As much as I wanted to make a commitment to this beautiful girl, I was terribly unsure of myself. I needed to know that I could and would stick to my commitment. Ginny showed me so much love and had such a submissive spirit, I knew I couldn't marry her unless I was sure her trust was well placed. I couldn't bear the thought of ever letting her down. I finally made up my mind. I would not make a commitment unless I was absolutely sure I could keep it. But I had no idea how to find that assurance. My spirit was in agony, and my mind was in turmoil.

Ginny said she understood, but I couldn't believe she did. Who but Ginny Lynn would continue to trust a man who said he loved her and wanted to marry her but couldn't until he was sure his commitment was greater than he was?

I needed help, which I sought from Mom and Dad. They were sympathetic and smart enough to point me to someone else. They suggested I talk with Dr. Wally Swanson and his wife, Charlotte. We had known them for years, and I knew they would offer honest advice. So I went.

After pouring out my heart to them and explaining in great detail the anguish of my uncertainty, I waited for their wonderful revelation. I really expected some secret revelation that had been withheld from me until this moment of initiation, the password that would grant me entrance to the world of stable and wise certainty. What I got instead seemed trite and unfeeling: "Ask the Lord to show you," they advised. "Only He knows what the future holds. If He blesses your commitment, you will know you can keep your word to love and cherish Virginia for as long as you live."

I could have given myself that advice without spending hours pouring out my heart before these people! As much as I respected and trusted them, I felt betrayed. Sure, we pray for God's blessing. Sure, we ask Him to show us His will. But He doesn't answer plainly. It's always a mystery. This was not some small matter to be treated casually. This was a pivotal moment in my life. For all I knew, all of history was at a crossroads. This was more important than life or death—this was gut-wrenching, heart-stopping, mind-numbing love.

I left the Swansons' house deflated. I had struck out. Worse yet, Ginny—sweet, trusting girl that she was—was waiting with great expectations for the outcome of our meeting. I was heading back empty handed.

Before I reached Mom and Dad's, I had a fleeting thought. Like a microscopic seed striving to root in untilled soil, it searched for a hold in my mind. Could it be that God *does* really answer prayers—not vaguely, but clearly and explicitly? Could He know the torment of my soul? Could it be that until now I had never needed His direction with sufficient urgency to merit a clear answer? What choice did I have, anyway?

"What did they tell you?" Ginny asked, eyes sparkling, when I showed up.

"They said we should ask God to show us if this is His will," I replied.

"Are we going to do it, then? How will we know if God answers?"

"I don't know. I have to be honest with you, Ginny," I confided. "I believe God exists, I believe He loves us, and I believe He gives guidance, but I don't have confidence that He will reveal His will to us like this. I won't be asking with the confidence James 1:6 says we must have. But I'm going to ask anyway. Let's ask together, and let's just hope He works a miracle for us and in us so we'll know our commitment will stand—not because we made it but because God blessed it and gave us the assurance it would last."

So we prayed. Together and separately. Every time I began to agonize, I would pray. My mind felt like jelly. I have never been *less* sure of myself than I was during those awful days of faithless waiting. I couldn't imagine why Ginny didn't want to pack up and go home. But she understood that the basis of my uncertainty was my determination to make a permanent, lifelong commitment to her.

I have heard people say they want to live together before marrying to be sure it will work. I always think that sort of a test is like tasting ice cream to evaluate whether working in an ice cream factory would be fun. But those days of agonizing—now *that* was a test—were miserable days. I didn't know how long I could last or what option I would have when I could no longer stand waiting for God to answer.

Then the answer came! No, it didn't really come; it was just suddenly there. Miraculously, wonderfully, unbelievably, God's answer—the assurance of His blessing and partnership—was there. I had envisioned handwriting on the wall or the appearance of a scroll with God's message on it. Instead He gave me a better, more appropriate answer. God's answer didn't tell me to ignore the uncertainty I felt in my own ability to make a lifelong commitment to love and cherish and protect and esteem Ginny. Instead He simply changed my constitution. Where I had wavered like a cattail in a breeze, turning to a different conclusion with every puff of wind, now I was suddenly steady. Where I had been like jelly in my resolve, now I was very sure. Where I had believed that only discipline could keep me to my intended vows, now I had a quiet, confident peace that God Himself would underwrite my pledge.

To adequately describe the wonderful release and the pleasure of the stability that I so desperately needed and received is beyond the power of my pen. Only those who have felt the gut-tearing and miserable uncertainty I experienced can truly understand the ecstasy of what I fully believe was God's intervention. Like real love itself, when I had God's answer, I knew I had it.

The first test of my blessed and incredible assurance was to tell Ginny. She wanted me to be sure, but she had seen me in the jelly state—she would know if this miracle resolve was just self-delusion. I knew my telling her what had happened would test the validity of the assurance. Thankfully, when I told Ginny, it was clear that she, too, could see the dramatic, miraculous change in me.

Whenever I tell this story, I can't help but think about how incredible it is that God intervened in a situation that was monumental to me but totally insignificant universally.

Ginny and I have been married thirty-three years now. It's not a coincidence that I am still sure. This is one of God's signs that the tides of time have not diminished in any way. Why God chose to answer my plea for help so wonderfully and explicitly I cannot tell. I have called out for help and direction often. I know He still guides me, but never again have I discovered a sand castle so intricately detailed and custom built on my beach. Mostly I see faint markings in the sand now and again, but I recognize the origin and know I have company on my island.

CHAPTER 2

OUT OF THE SKY ◂

It was all over the news. The value of the Mexican peso had dropped into the basement overnight. This doesn't happen in the United States, where our economy is incredibly stable, but it does happen in third world countries.

When I heard the news about the peso, I called a friend I had grown up with in Ecuador. We had also been college roommates and had stayed in close touch since graduating. We had both done a bit of import/export business with Ecuadorean goods, and I told him that I thought this might be a good time to visit Mexico to see if any business opportunities would arise ut of this economic upheaval south of the border. By this time, Ginny and I were married and living in Minnesota, so we decided that I would fly my plane from Minnesota down to Little Rock, Arkansas, where Jimmy would fly in to meet me. From there, we would fly together to Mexico.

Everything went pretty well until we got to Texas. We were

following the Gulf Coast and had just about reached Corpus Christi. It was getting a bit hazy outside, but I didn't worry about it. I had learned to fly in an old World War II vintage trainer that didn't even have a starter or a radio. By comparison, my Cessna 172 had two radios, navigation aids, an artificial horizon, and other modern instruments. I did not have a rating that would allow me to fly purely by instruments, but the weather was far from requiring that as yet.

Then without any warning at all, the sky became opaque. The outside temperature had dropped to the dew point, and all the moisture in the air had suddenly turned to clouds. We were just beginning to cross the bay north of Corpus Christi. The only view I had was straight down, and I knew we were in trouble.

If you aren't used to flying by reference to instruments, it is extremely easy to get vertigo. Your natural sense of balance gets disoriented, and your mind tells you that you are level when you are actually turning, or that you are turning when you are actually level. It takes practice and discipline to believe what the instruments are saying and to ignore the powerful instincts that tell you they are wrong. I did not dare take my eyes off of the instruments.

Trying to keep my voice calm, I told Jimmy that we needed to get on the ground immediately. "I saw a small airstrip on the map right on the north shore of the bay. Look down and see if you can find it!" I yelled over the roar of the engine, trying to cover the rising panic in my voice.

"Yeah, I think that's an airstrip right below us," Jimmy replied almost immediately. I took my eyes off the instruments and looked down. Sure enough, there was a small airstrip exactly below us. I banked into a steep turn, keeping my eyes on that little strip of asphalt. With the power completely off and the flaps all the way out in a steep turn, we were spiraling down toward the ground. I leveled the wings at the last minute just before plunging into Corpus Christi Bay, shooting over the shoreline to a very comforting short-field landing at the small airfield in Portland, Texas.

As Jimmy and I taxied up to the tiny terminal, we were met by a red-haired young man in a leather flying jacket. "Boy, you guys sure chose some crummy weather to visit Portland in," the stranger commented.

"Well, the visibility was fine until just a few minutes ago," I replied defensively.

"Yeah, that happens around the bay on a fairly regular basis. You guys must not be from around here."

The muscular redhead fueled us up so that we would be ready to leave whenever the weather cleared up. I had just signed the fuel ticket when he asked where we were headed.

"We're heading for Mexico," Jimmy answered. The young man, whose name was also Steve, turned out to be the local pilot, flight instructor, and airport manager. He told us we shouldn't really plan to fly into Mexico unless we spoke Spanish.

"We both grew up in Ecuador and speak Spanish," I informed him, feeling a little uneasy that he was being so nosy. When we were done tying the plane down and were ready to leave the airfield, Steve asked us where we were planning to stay. We hadn't planned for the weather to suddenly change. We hadn't planned to stop in Portland, "Nowhere," Texas, and of course, we had not planned for a place to stay.

"It's a long way into Corpus," Steve told us, "and there aren't any motels in Portland. But if you don't mind staying with a fornicator, you can stay with my girlfriend and me—we have a little place just a few blocks away."

Something was odd about Steve Davis. First, he had aggressively nosed into our personal affairs, and now he was giving us unnecessary personal information about himself. But he *was* offering us a roof over our heads for the night, and Jimmy and I were willing to overlook a lot if it meant we wouldn't have to sleep on the cold floor of the tiny airport-terminal shack.

Steve's girlfriend, Linda, showed up shortly after we arrived at his rental house. She seemed to be about as surprised that Steve had invited us to stay with them as I had been. Something strange was going on, but as long as we were warm, dry, and fed, I didn't want to rock the boat. Turns out I didn't have to. Steve took care of that.

As soon as we returned from getting some barbecue down the street, Steve put some old Elvis Presley gospel records on the turntable. He had the record player turned up so loud that we couldn't help but listen. That wasn't so odd, but what was odd were the snide remarks Steve was making about the song's lyrics. The longer the music played, the more cynical and derogatory Steve's comments became. I couldn't help but wonder what had made this redheaded flyboy so hypersensitive about music he *chose* to listen to.

"Can you believe people actually believe this stuff?" Steve asked. "They are just a bunch of hypocrites. They need a crutch to get through life, so they pretend that God exists and that He personally cares about them. People who believe that are just a bunch of losers." He went on and on. I wondered if I should admit that I was one of those "crutch-needing hypocrites" or if I should just let it ride until he had blown off some steam.

I woke up early the next morning, ready to fly out of Portland, Texas, and away from Steve Davis forever. But when I looked outside, I could hardly make out the house across the street through the incredibly dense fog. Jimmy and I couldn't go anywhere, and Steve had to cancel his flying students, so we spent the entire day together. It was miserable. Steve went out of his way to denigrate everything I held spiritually important in life.

I tried to interject a few times and say that I believed most of what he was making fun of. But Steve was not looking for a discussion. He just spewed venom against the very idea of God's existence, and even more against the idea that God might actually intervene in the personal lives of individual people. I got the impression that although Steve did believe what he was saying, for some inexplicable reason, our presence in his home had sparked his nonstop commentary.

By the end of the day, I was fed up with the tirade against God that Steve was determined to subject us to. Worse yet, he seemed to aim most of his comments at me. I couldn't wait for the sun to come up the next morning. Steve had assured us that the fog usually lasted a few hours to a day at most. I was sure that the sky would be crystal clear the second morning.

But it wasn't. If anything, it was worse than the day before. I had never seen such dense fog. We couldn't fly; that was clear. But I wasn't going to spend another day listening to Steve Davis rail against God and anyone who believed in Him as a caring, powerful, personal Creator. I was ready to walk to Mexico if necessary.

Steve agreed to give us a ride out to the main road. There, Jimmy and I stuck out our thumbs to hitchhike to Mexico. I hated to leave the plane behind, but I absolutely couldn't take any more of Steve's ranting. We got a ride in the back of a pickup, where we scrunched under an old topper and headed south.

Just south of Corpus, as we were driving through the huge King Ranch, the sky suddenly became clear. The temperature had finally risen above the dew point, and all of the water vapor in the air evaporated just as quickly as it had condensed two days before.

Jimmy and I banged on the cab and told our surprised driver that we had changed our minds. Out in the middle of nowhere, we stuck out our thumbs again on the other side of the road, in an attempt to get back to Portland. We quickly found a ride from a Marine who was on leave. He was heading north on the main road but wasn't in a hurry, so he offered to drive us back into the "boonies" to Steve and Linda's house. I did not want to see Steve Davis again, so I asked the Marine if he would drop Jimmy at the house to get the rest of our gear, and then drive me out to get the plane ready for the flight to Mexico. He agreed and drove me right past the little terminal and out to my plane.

After he left, I started untying the plane as quickly as I could. I was double-checking that the plane's tanks were full when Steve saw me. He yelled something that sounded like, "Hey, Steve, guess what? Linda and I are going to serve the Lord."

This time he had crossed the line. I had taken all I was going to take. I decided that if he came over to the plane, I was going to hit him right in the nose. The last time I had done that was in grade school when another boy made some denigrating comments about my mother. Now here I was, a grown Christian man, contemplating hitting someone who had made it abundantly clear that he had a chip on his shoulder against anyone who believed in God.

I hate to even admit that the idea of hitting Steve occurred to me, except to emphasize the fact that Steve's persistent and demeaning comments about God had driven me past the point of rationality. Steve was a big guy, and I got the idea that he had a little more experience with hitting people than I did. I guess I felt it was a matter of honor that I defend God. I did not have time to think through the idea very well, or it would have been clear to me that if I tried to defend God, He would certainly have to defend me in return.

My fears were coming true. Steve Davis was heading for me. But just then, Linda roared around the flight shack in Steve's "ghetto cruiser" and came to a skidding stop in a cloud of dust in front of my plane. She jumped out and ran toward me with a strange look on her face. Before I could react, she threw her arms around me and exclaimed, "You'll never believe what has happened. Steve and I have decided we are going to serve God."

I didn't know what to think. Linda had not tried to stop Steve's biting and nasty comments against spiritual things, but she had not joined in the mockery until now. But as soon as Linda let go of me, I took a closer look at her. She was doing that girl thing—half crying and half laughing—that Ginny had been trying to teach me about for several years.

By then, Steve had reached us, and he and Linda began to explain what was happening. There *was* a lot more to their story. Steve had grown up in Mexico, where his mother and father were Christian missionaries. But Steve's father betrayed Steve, his mother, and his younger sister, running away with another woman—away from them and from God and his missionary work.

Steve, too, had turned his back on God, blaming Him for allowing his family to be ruined. He also turned on the church for being a bunch of hypocrites who pretended to believe something that they didn't really live. He wanted nothing to do with spiritual things. Linda had grown up in a Christian home of a different sort. Her parents had attended church, but they did not let spiritual beliefs affect their personal lives in an open and transparent way. Linda found her joy in music and played the oboe professionally. She also found love at an early age and got married. But the marriage was on the rocks almost as soon as it started. While Steve wondered if God even existed, Linda decided He just didn't care.

When Steve and Linda met and started comparing notes, they realized they shared a common cynicism for God and spiritual things. After they began living together, Steve told Linda that the only spiritual thing he could not easily discount was something mystical that had happened to him as a boy.

Steve's father, like mine, was a pilot—and like me, Steve became fascinated by airplanes at an early age. Before their family's traumatic breakup, Steve's mother bought him a book titled *Through Gates of Splendor*. Steve read the book and became captivated by the story of Jim Elliot, Roger Youderian, Pete Fleming, Ed McCully, and my dad, Nate Saint. He felt a supernatural touch and the assurance that one day he, too, would grow up to be a missionary pilot.

When Steve and his dad would fly over the Mexican countryside, his dad sometimes allowed Steve to take the controls while he pretended to catch a few winks. In those special moments at the controls, Steve pictured himself as the next Nate Saint, "Jungle Pilot."

But when Steve's dad made it apparent by his actions that what he had preached was more show than substance, it profoundly discouraged Steve. He finally concluded that he could not live life perfectly to meet God's standards, so he gave up. Steve also gave up the dream of serving God as a missionary pilot. Even then, he could not explain away the mystical experience he had had while reading *Through Gates of Splendor.*

Together, Steve and Linda decided to challenge God, if He existed, to reveal Himself to them. They challenged God, if He cared about them, to bring someone they would know was specifically sent to convince them that He does exist and does care. If God did that, they decided they would believe in Him. If not, they were finished with God. Steve told me that when I had signed the fuel ticket, he had recognized my last name. He remembered from *Through Gates of Splendor* that Nate Saint also had a son named Steve. In fact, he had just recently pulled his dusty old copy of the book out of storage and had once again looked at the picture of me, the "other Steve," with my pet parrot. Steve told Linda, "I'll bet the Steve in the book is in worse spiritual condition than I am."

As Steve Davis viewed that picture, he remembered the story that had captured his heart and his imagination. He concluded again that the jungle pilot's son must have also figured out that Christianity was just a hoax, something people went along with for the sake of tradition.

Finding it hard to believe that the boy in the book had actually landed in Podunk Portland, Texas, Steve decided to test me. That's when he made his comments about needing to speak Spanish in Mexico. When he realized that this really *was* that other Steve, he wanted to find out what, if anything, his counterpart believed about God.

It wasn't until after Jimmy and I left that Linda confronted Steve. "We challenged God to send someone specifically to us as proof that He exists and that He cares for us personally. If

Nate Saint's son isn't the messenger we have been looking for, there never will be one. Now it is time to believe or shut the door forever."

The implications were huge, whichever way they turned. If they turned their backs on God for good, the implications would be eternal. But if they turned to God, "then we have to stop living together, and we've got to get married," Steve said. "And then I will have to forgive my dad for what he did to Mom and our family. And then we will have to live our lives in line with God's plan and serve Him."

As Steve was finishing the story, Linda looked like she was going to explode. "So that is just what we are going to do," Linda said. "We are going to serve the Lord."

Steve chimed in, "I have already moved out of the house, and Linda and I are going to get married. But first, I have to go see my dad. I have to forgive him and ask his blessing before Linda and I get married."

Steve and Linda have stayed in touch with me for three decades now. Steve did forgive his dad and has maintained contact with him. He and Linda have lived consistent lives of faith in God and service to Him since God answered their challenge. Steve is now a pilot with American Eagle, and he and Linda frequently fly to Mexico to encourage and help God followers there.

About ten years after I met Steve and Linda, they called with the happy news that they were going to have a baby. Steve told me they had chosen a special name. "We are going to call her Stephenie Saint Davis. But don't get a big head. We are commemorating what God used you to do for us. It doesn't really have much to do with you." Steve chuckled. He was worried that I would get an inflated view of myself. But I knew what this was about. It was just another sign of God along life's trail to let us know that He really does exist and that He very definitely cares.[1]

CHAPTER 3

SILK PURSES

They say that you can't make a silk purse out of a sow's ear. Says who? I've seen some situations in life that sure looked like tough, bristly old sows' ears, and in the end they turned out to be pretty smooth and elegant.

I once read about a woman who was statutorily raped and became pregnant. The rapist knew that since her husband had been away at war, he would know that he wasn't the father. So the rapist had the husband killed. The woman didn't even press charges. For one thing, she didn't want to advertise her son's illegitimacy. She also knew that the man who took advantage of her was well connected, and there was no way he would ever be convicted.

It seemed like a hopeless situation, but in the end, God blessed this woman richly. One of her sons even grew up to be the richest, most powerful man alive. And I have read that he was also the wisest dude of his day too. You can read more about this great story in 2 Samuel, beginning with chapter 11.

But what about the situations where it seems impossible that the outcome can be good? Ginny recently read a true story about a model young man who married a divorced woman with two young daughters. He loved the two girls as though they were his own. But the biological father decided that he wanted to start spending time with his daughters, even though he had totally abandoned them up to that point. The mother was terrified that the biological father would abuse her precious girls.

The stepfather tried to reason with the biological father, but when he, too, was convinced that this man would hurt the girls, he felt he had no alternative but to kill him. Today that man is in a penitentiary about eighty miles from where I sit writing. He will never be free again. This is one of those sow's ears that looks as if it will stay a sow's ear.

But that is just the point. Sometimes in life we face messy situations that nothing will ever make right. And then God steps in and turns the situations around so that they have happy endings, or at least so that the mess makes sense and has purpose.

Those turnarounds make for some of the most important stories we can pass on to our descendents. They are faith builders. Once we see enough of those God signs, our faith becomes strong and steady, and we can believe that things are going to be okay even when all the evidence points to the contrary. We know this because "faith is the confidence that what we hope for will actually happen; it gives us assurance about things we cannot see" (Hebrews 11:1).

I'm not talking about forcing a smile as the guillotine blade falls. I'm talking about really believing that God can stop the blade, and that if He doesn't, He must have a better plan. Consider William Tyndale, who was burned at the stake for believing that the Scriptures are true and that common people should have access to the Bible in their own language. His final prayers included a request that God would move the king, under whose authority he was condemned and being executed, to allow the Scriptures to be made available. Henry VIII did exactly that, but not before Tyndale was martyred. I'm sure to anyone watching, Tyndale's execution seemed like a sow's ear. But the result was the great spiritual awakening of England. That was exactly the silk purse William Tyndale hoped for. His greatest wish came true as a result of his death.

There is also a sow's ear–silk purse story within the story that I am so closely associated with.

After my dad and his four friends were killed, three Waodani women walked out of the jungle into a Quechua settlement. The Quechua women who first saw these naked apparitions screamed in fear, and their husbands ran to get their muzzle-loading shotguns. But the Waodani women were not killed.

Betty Elliot, Jim's widow, happened to be just a couple of hours away by trail. She was notified and went immediately to see the women. By the time she got to where they were, one of the women, Dawa, had already disappeared back into the jungle, where her husband was hiding and waiting for her. Aunt Betty took the other two women back to her mission station, where they would be safe. She knew that if they stayed in the community where they had appeared, it was highly probable that someone would attempt to kill them in retaliation for Quechua family members who had been speared by the Waodani. Shandia, where Aunt Betty lived, was farther from

31

Waodani territory, so fewer people there had personal vendettas against the Waodani.

Mintaka and Mangamo spent months with Aunt Betty and her daughter, Valerie. My dad's sister, Rachel, was in the United States at the time with Dayumae, a Waodani woman who had fled from her people for fear of her life years before. When Aunt Rachel and Dayumae returned to Ecuador, they realized that not only were Mintaka and Mangamo from Dayumae's clan, they were her very own aunts. When Mintaka and Mangamo saw that their niece was still alive, they were amazed. The Waodani had no social institution or individual with the authority to stop the rampant killing that had eroded their once significant tribe to the fragile fringes of extinction.

Mintaka and Mangamo insisted that Dayumae return with them so she could explain how some of the foreigners had learned to live without hating and killing each other. She agreed, and they were back in less than a month with a delegation of Waodani who invited Aunt Rachel and Aunt Betty to return with them.

That part of the story is common knowledge. What is not commonly known is that Aunt Rachel did not really want Aunt Betty to go in with her. Aunt Rachel was convinced that this was her assignment from God. God had given her a vision as a teenager in which He promised that if she was faithful to Him, He would allow her to take His Word to a people who had never heard of Him. From the time my dad first informed her of the violent "Aucas," she knew that these were the people God had promised she would take His message to.

And besides, she had already been studying the Waodani language with Dayumae. Aunt Betty had only spent a couple of months with Mintaka and Mangamo. They could not help

Aunt Betty learn much of their language because, unlike Dayu-mae, they did not understand Quechua.

Aunt Betty, on the other hand, did not think it was a good idea for Aunt Rachel, who was already in her midforties, to be part of a new attempt to make contact. Everyone knew that if you walked into Waodani territory, you would have to walk back out, too. Because of the extreme topography of Waodani territory, it would have been nearly impossible to carry someone like Aunt Rachel—or Aunt Betty, for that matter—out of the jungle if she wasn't able to make it on her own. Under the best of circumstances, it might have taken most of a week.

Neither of them thought the other should go in. They were both strong women with definite opinions. Their spiritual commitment was very similar: They were both willing to put everything they had—even their very lives—on the line if they thought obeying God required it. But many of their other opinions were different.

Aunt Betty grew up in a very organized and rigid home. The Howards spoke precise English and obeyed precise rules. Expectations were high, meals were served on a set schedule, and family rules were not open to debate.

My grandparents' house where Dad and Aunt Rachel grew up was very different. Granddad was an artist and Grandmother was an art connoisseur. They had artistic temperaments. You ate when you were hungry or when Grandma Saint served the next meal. When Dad and his brothers decided to sleep on the roof of their three-story house, Grandma joined them. When Dad decided to disassemble the family car to see what made it tick, he was only expected to get it back together before Grandpa had to deliver his next stained glass window. One professional writing team commented that if Aunt Rachel and

Aunt Betty had had psychological evaluations before going to the tribe, probably no group would ever have tried to put their two highly motivated, independent personalities together.[2]

Here is where God's intervention in what should have ended in a major personality explosion appeared. Aunt Betty finally asked that Aunt Rachel prove that she could handle the tough physical requirements of the long trek into Waodani territory. I think she really thought that Aunt Rachel would not be able to make it. But I also think that Aunt Betty figured it would be best if she went alone. When Rachel heard that she might need to prove she could make the demanding journey, her response was this: "I will not put God to the test unnecessarily. If He wants me to live with the 'Aucas,' He will give me the strength I need when I need it."

When I read Aunt Rachel's journals after her death, it created a crisis in my own heart. I had no idea that there had been such severe disagreement and discord between these two women whom I had loved and respected all my life. Aunt Betty was an intellectual. Her interests were broad, and she read widely ranging subjects to satisfy that intellectual appetite. When Aunt Rachel found that Aunt Betty was reading Nietzsche while Aunt Rachel was trying to give the Waodani God's Word as a basis for stopping the genocide within their tribe, she was outraged. Aunt Betty thought that they had to take a slow but steady approach in trying to explain God's carvings to the Waodani. She wanted to be sure they did not get something wrong and have to go back and straighten it out. But Aunt Rachel was desperate to give everyone a chance to understand God's trail before there were more killings and some precious Waodani lost that chance forever.

I could go on and on about the contrasts between Betty

and Rachel. Suffice it to say, it is a wonder that there wasn't a huge explosion out there in the Ecuadorean Amazon. I know that both women were hurt by the other's lack of acceptance. But God works through hurt. In fact, He rarely works through our joy. It is pain that God uses to mold and make us people He can use. Divine joy proves itself when it exists in spite of suffering.

At first, learning of the strong tensions between these two godly women I respected so much created a spiritual dilemma for me. But here is my conclusion: God wanted Betty *and* Rachel to live with the Waodani, but He didn't want them both to stay.

God used Aunt Betty's involvement with the Waodani to give her great exposure and high credibility in the Christian world. And there can be no debate that He has used her to influence hundreds of thousands of women and men through her syndicated radio program as well as her powerful speaking, insightful writing, and wise counsel.

Aunt Rachel never could have done what Aunt Betty did. But neither could Aunt Betty have done what Aunt Rachel did, giving up her life to the Waodani, adapting to their culture and living with them for thirty-six years.

I love many of the Waodani. Some of them are as much family to me as my own flesh and blood. But they are a difficult people to live with. Their culture has no authority. There is no law, no law enforcement, and no concept of corporate punishment or reward. Living with the Waodani is like living in a soap opera on fast-forward.

From the first day she went to live with them until the day she died, Aunt Rachel loved the Waodani, their culture, their customs, their food, and their idiosyncrasies. In fact, when she was dying, she even reverted to speaking their language, Wao-Tededo. This is highly unusual since multilingual people almost without exception revert to their mother tongue when they are close to death. Aunt Rachel never considered living with the Waodani her work. She thought of it as her reward for being obedient to God's assignments in her life.

My conclusion is simply this: God took two strong-willed women who struggled to get along, and used them for His purposes. If you stopped the story at the point where Betty and Rachel realized they simply could not tolerate each other in civility any longer, you would have a sow's ear. But the next few chapters, written by the Master Scribe, show that this story is truly a silk purse.

Thousands of people have told me what heroes of the faith both Aunt Betty and Aunt Rachel have been to them. I know they are both my heroes. Their stories are sand castles in my life and God signs on my own personal trail. And their story convinces me once more that God cares and has a plan. We just need to listen and obey, allowing Him to write the story.

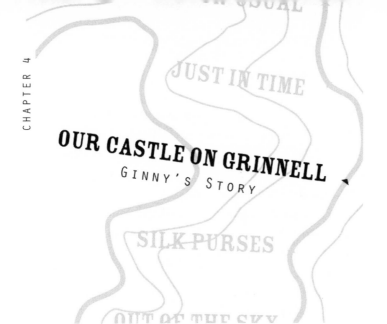

CHAPTER 4

OUR CASTLE ON GRINNELL
GINNY'S STORY

A house is not just a house; it's so much more—or at least it can be.

There's an old saying that is frequently printed on mugs, T-shirts, and needlepoint wall hangings: If mama ain't happy, ain't nobody happy. And if this mama doesn't have a home, be it ever so humble, this mama ain't happy.

When Steve is out speaking, people often ask him where home is. He usually answers, "We have one house in Florida and one house down in the jungles of Ecuador." Then he always adds, "But for me, home is where Ginny is." Well, Ginny can be happy almost anywhere for a period of time, but to be settled, I need a house to make into a home.

The first home I remember while growing up was a house in the country with apple trees and a cherry tree that was great for climbing, a chicken coop, and an old abandoned outhouse that mom didn't like us playing in, for reasons that seem obvious now. We also had three acres to explore and a railroad track that added all kinds of excitement.

It was fairly traumatic when we had to move into the "city," a town of about ten thousand people. But the big old two-story house on Second Street in Willmar also became home after a few years. I finished grade school there and suffered through the emotions of adolescence and junior high in that house. It was my home through high school and junior college. And when I went down to "the Cities" (Minneapolis–St. Paul) for nursing school, that grand old house with the slide-down banister was still home.

It was at that house that Steve came to meet my family before whisking me off to Ecuador for adventures that I never could have anticipated. Except for the few years we lived out in the country, that big white house in town was my home for the first twenty-two years of my life. When I moved with Steve to Ecuador, it was the first time in my twenty-two years that I had ever really lived away from home.

I lived with Steve's parents for three months until we got married, then in a missionary senoritas' apartment building for two months while we were early honeymooners.

After that, we moved out of Quito to live in the houses Steve was building in the country for his parents and other missionaries. We lived in various parts of those houses while they were built around us for the next nine months.

When we returned to the States, we spent an entire month in Willmar decompressing from the day-and-night schedule of Steve's construction business in Ecuador. During that month in Willmar, Steve tried to figure out what to do next while I just reveled in being "home."

We decided to move to Wheaton, Illinois, to see if there were any opportunities for Steve to use his bilingual and tricultural background in missions or some other type of ministry. Nothing opened up there, but an old friend of his family in Grand Rapids, Michigan, needed help building up a new kitchen-remodeling business to complement his tile-and-flooring business. So we moved to Grand Rapids, where home became a second-story apartment with no memories and no character.

After being in Grand Rapids for only a month and a half, we found out that my dad had brain cancer, so we headed back to Willmar. We moved in with Mom to help with Dad and my younger siblings who were still at home. Steve started a kitchen-remodeling business similar to the one he had helped with in Grand Rapids. My dad died five months later.

After we were sure that Mom would be okay, Steve accepted a management job in a Minneapolis hospital. We spent a year there in a rented apartment, but it didn't take us long to figure out that Steve wasn't a good fit for managing a team of union employees.

After that whirlwind tour, even Steve felt some need to be settled. Living in seven different homes on two continents and three states in just under three years had taken its toll. We did not feel God's leading to go anyplace in particular, so we headed back to Willmar.

I was incredibly happy being a wife to Steve and a new mother to our first son, Shaun Felipe. My job was to take care of Steve and Shaun and work as a nurse from time to time. But I was not sure where we belonged, and neither was Steve. That was what made Willmar so attractive to us.

My mom and nearly all of my five brothers and sisters and their wives and husbands and children were still there at the time. And, although we didn't yet know it, Steve's brother,

Phil, would soon accept a position to teach in a new Christian school in Willmar, so even some of Steve's family would be in town! When we first returned to Willmar, we lived in a tiny apartment under the eaves on the second story of an old house. That apartment sure had a lot of personality. To sit down, you had to back into the couch under the sloping ceiling. And in the dead of Minnesota winter, our only heat was an oil-burning stove in the middle of the tiny kitchen floor. One night when I woke up to nurse Shaun, I realized that our bedroom door had swung closed. Shaun's blankets were covered in frost, and we thought for an instant that he had frozen to death. But he was still cuddly warm, thanks to several layers of blankets under the frost-laden top cover. In spite of its quirks, this apartment was in a place where I felt I belonged, which made it "home" in a way that the apartments in Wheaton, Grand Rapids, and Minneapolis had not been.

After a while, we moved to a house that needed to be remodeled so it could be sold. Steve did the remodeling in exchange for rent while he started to build a construction company. By the time he had that house remodeled, he also had two new houses built, and Jaime Nate Mincaye had joined our family.

Steve sold one of our new houses, and we moved into the other one. This house really became home for me. Not only was the house ours, but it was in a town that was "ours" too.

Some houses are just houses. But other houses become home. There is a huge difference between the two. Men don't naturally understand this. That is one of the things that we women have to help them with.

Shortly after we were married, Steve was talking about his

thoughts and plans for the future. He just casually mentioned that he couldn't imagine living in one place for more than a whole year. Then he rolled over and went to sleep. Any tendency I had toward sleep was long gone. I wondered just how much adventure this hometown girl was going to get in the bargain I had made with this man I had fallen so completely in love with. It is amazing that that same man was able to live happily in Willmar for almost seven years. Steve frequently tells people that he had to do seven years for me like Jacob had to give seven years for Rachel. Then, with a twinkle in his eye, he adds, "That is why I only married one of the Olson sisters."

Yeah, likely story. Neither of my sisters would have had him! They are both happily married and have never really lived anywhere but Willmar—and they still have no plans to leave. They love Steve, but they have made it very clear that they could not have lived the life that we have, including all of the moves. Of course, they have never gotten to live with Steve, either, so they wouldn't understand.

———

Steve joined his construction business with Forry, a man he served with on the board of the local Christian school. The business grew in spite of the terrible recession we were in. At the time, mortgage rates were climbing as high as 17 percent.

Forry had lost his first wife and one of his two boys in a terrible blizzard just about the time we first moved to Willmar. One day Forry told Steve that losing his wife and son had dampened his desire to work day and night as the residential construction business tends to demand.

"I'm getting out," he told Steve. "Do you want to buy me out or get out with me?"

I had complete confidence in Steve and his decisions. He had proven that he could provide for us, and he cared about my feelings. And I knew that he wanted our lives to count for more than just building a net worth or enjoying the American Dream. That was one of the things that had attracted me to Steve.

I did not feel strongly either way about staying in construction or doing something entirely different. Steve, however, reminded me of something a close friend of ours had recently said. Mary had a big family and an even bigger backyard, although the yard was a disaster: Bare spots protruded from shabby grass where her kids had made bases or decided to dig a mud pit. But Mary wasn't concerned. She simply said, "You can have happy kids or grass. We decided in favor of happy kids."

Steve said he thought it was the same with children and construction. As long as we had children at home, he wanted to be there for them, and without a partner, he knew he'd have to devote a lot more time to the business than he had been. So we decided to sell our business with Forry and do something else—even though we weren't sure what that might be.

A close friend of Steve's from Orlando asked him to consider joining his oil and gas exploration business in Texas. This friend, J. Steven, and his dad had been drilling oil wells in Ohio for years, but they wanted to get into the bigger upside potential in West Texas and Oklahoma.

J. Steven's brothers, who were also part of the family business, needed to stay in Florida, so J. Steven wanted Steve to be his right-hand man in the new venture in Texas. Steve would be a partner, but the buck would not stop at his desk. That was a plus. We would have to move to Dallas, a glitzy big city where we wouldn't know anyone except J. Steven and his family.

It would mean finding a new house and making it home. By this time, we had added Jesse and Stephenie to our growing family. There would be six of us to move. I did not look forward to that, but surprisingly I did not dread it either. The secret would be for us to find just the right house, one that fit us and could quickly become home.

Steve flew off to spend a week in Dallas with J. Steven and his dad. They looked for offices and checked out houses and schools—all those things that complicate life in North America. When Steve called me, he was disheartened. Knowing we were moving to a big city where he would be dealing with wealthy investors, Steve had sold his pickup truck and bought a car we thought would fit better in Dallas. It was the most beautiful car we could imagine: a gray New Yorker with a tufted gray leather interior. Neither of us liked spending more money than necessary on cars, but we knew that not having a nice car would be an impediment to Steve's being taken seriously in his new work in Dallas.

When he called from Dallas, however, Steve told me that our beautiful, luxurious new car barely fit the minimum standard in Dallas. In Willmar, people had actually stopped to check out that car. Boy, was I in for an adjustment.

I flew down for a few days to join Steve in the house hunt. When I arrived, I quickly began to realize what he had been talking about. The difference between living just inside or outside the Dallas Beltway made a huge difference in price. And then there was the traffic issue. Even if you lived close to where you worked, it could take an hour or more to get there. Or you could live further out but only spend half that time getting to work. It all depended on what roads you had to use, what time of the day you had to drive, and which direction you were going. Those were issues I had never had to deal with in Willmar.

What if we made the wrong choice? Steve and I had decided to live modestly so we could pay for our house with cash. Could we do that in Dallas? Should we borrow money and live close to Steve's work, or stick with our game plan to be debt free?

We went to see some houses and found that they were all pretty much the same. The style was not what we were used to at all. The yards were all very tiny and fenced in, which gave a bit of privacy but made me feel cut off from our neighbors.

The houses we looked at were nice, but somehow I couldn't see any of them as a home for Steph, Jesse, Jaime, Shaun, Steve, and me. They were expensive, too, compared to what we were used to.

Finally we drove over to see another neighborhood Steve had heard about. On the way, we passed what seemed to be a scene from rural Minnesota. On one side of the busy street we were on sat a bunch of mini farms, each one with a small, old house on it. There were goats on one property and what looked like fruit trees on another one. A couple of the plots were tilled and ready for planting.

Now, we could handle this, I thought. *Our kids could grow up like I did.*

But Steve had already checked it out. Those properties were all going to be turned into high-density housing developments as soon as the last one or two property owners decided to get on board. No one could sell unless everyone agreed. And we may have been able to buy an acre in one corner, but we wouldn't have had any money left to build our house. We kept on going.

In most of the neighborhoods we drove through, I got a knot in my stomach. I just could not imagine any of them being home. As Steve and I drove into the last neighborhood, the knot went away, although I didn't know why. The houses looked the same as those we had already seen. I couldn't tell visibly that anything was different.

As Steve drove down a street in this new neighborhood, I saw one lone two-story house sticking up between the forest of houses that were so wide they filled nearly every bit of their lots. *Oh, if only that one were available,* I thought, although I didn't say anything to Steve as we drove up. What were the chances it would be for sale?

But it was! As Steve started to drive by, I asked him to stop so we could write down the telephone number on the sign.

"There are good reasons why people don't build two-story houses in this area," Steve said. He went on to tell me about how the ground could dry out under the foundations if you didn't water them.

If you didn't water the foundations? Our home in Willmar was built on land that once was a slough. If your sump pump quit, your basement would fill with water. Surely Steve didn't mean that you had to water your foundations here.

My heart was beating fast. Even if we had to water the foundation, surely this house was way out of our price range. It was so bright and airy and high. The smaller footprint of the two-story design left a lot more yard than typical Dallas one-story houses did.

When the real estate agent let us in the next morning, just before I had to return to Minnesota, Steve immediately noticed water spots on a couple of the room's ceilings. He was concerned about that, as well as the age of the appliances and air conditioner compressors. I just wanted to explore.

With my first look, I just knew this was our house. It felt like a little corner of Minnesota in Dallas. The size was right, and the number of bedrooms and bathrooms was perfect. It had a front porch, just like I had always wanted. And the shutters were smoky blue, my color.

Steve took me aside where the real estate agent couldn't hear us and said, "Don't make it so obvious that you like it. The real estate agent works for the sellers. When the owners hear how much you like this house, the price will probably go up."

"What is the price?" I asked Steve. I was worried that the price would kill the deal. This house was so much nicer than what I had seen in the books Steve had sent to me, and what we had looked at together. I was sure it could not be in the same price range as the houses around it.

But when the real estate agent told us the asking price, it was actually quite reasonable. I couldn't believe it. *That must be a mistake,* I thought. *Or something serious is wrong with it.* I thought about Steve's initial comments about possible foundation problems. Maybe the house was just about to capsize because the foundation sprinklers didn't come on or something.

Steve interjected, "I think the price may be low because this isn't the style of house that people want to buy here in Dallas."

As he was talking, we rounded the corner into a small but cozy family room with a brick fireplace. That's when I got my confirmation that this was going to be our new home—not just our house but our *home.* In the corner of the family room was a Kirby vacuum cleaner. It was just like mine, even the same color, burgundy. And it was still plugged in, like it was just waiting for me.

I knew what had happened: God had kept this house for us. It had been on the market long enough that the sellers' employer had taken it over and reduced the price. And the real estate agent told us they even had a little more room to come down if we wanted to buy it soon.

The backyard had no pool. It wasn't even landscaped. It just had one tree and grass inside the typical backyard fence. *Perfect.* We didn't need elaborate landscaping; what we needed was a place for creative, energetic kids to play. The single tree was just big enough that I could climb it with the kids. I could not wait.

When we finished our tour of the house, we walked back out front, and I just knew that this was our house. But I could tell that Steve did not agree. He wasn't opposed to buying "my" house, but he wanted to be sure it was the right one.

I wanted this house. I had never felt this way about any other house. I felt if God had picked this one specifically for us, I knew He could make Steve feel the same way about it. As soon as I got back to Minnesota, Steve called to say he had decided to fast until the decision of buying a house was settled. Up to this point, we hadn't fasted very often and never for more than a couple of days. It really meant a lot to me that Steve was concerned enough about the house we were going to live in to fast and pray about it. I told him I would do the same. Well, almost the same. Steve was praying that God would show him. I was also praying that God would show him. I wanted Him to show Steve what I was sure He had already showed me.

Five days later, Steve called and told me, "You have your house." He had done some careful research and could not find any reason the house had not sold at its asking price, much less at the reduced price. And the sellers' company had even come down some more. They wanted to get it off their hands as quickly as possible. We had our house!

Now I began to wonder about the neighborhood.

We had seen some signs of kids in the neighborhood—a bicycle on the sidewalk and a stroller outside someone's house—but no hard evidence. Our four kids wanted to know if there was going to be anyone to play with.

We got our answer as we drove up with our U-Haul truck. It looked like a summer day camp. There were kids everywhere, and a lot of them seemed to be about the ages of our four. We had heard that neighbors in Dallas kept to themselves, but Grinnell Street did not fit that stereotype. Neighbors started appearing at our door with cookies and offers of help as soon as we pulled up. A little fellow from across the street came up to me with his hand extended.

"Hi, everyone, my name is Kyle, and I'm going to be your neighbor." He was so cute! And he did turn out to be a good neighbor too.

As we were unloading, Steve went out to get something from the moving truck. As he approached the truck, he noticed a woman just standing on the sidewalk looking at the house. She called him over.

Her name was Linda, and she lived in the house next to Kyle's.

"So you are going to be our new neighbors," she said. "What is your name?" Steve told her his name was Steve, but she didn't respond. So he continued. "My wife is Ginny, and we have four children: Shaun, Jaime, Stephenie, and Jesse." She appeared to be waiting for more information.

"We are the Saints," Steve finally said. At this, the woman raised her hands in the air and fell to her knees. She was looking up into the sky, not at Steve.

"Oh thank you, thank you," she exclaimed, so that anyone nearby could hear her. Then she looked back at Steve and explained emotionally, "I just knew you would be saints. I have been praying for months that this house would be bought by saints."

Steve was feeling a bit nervous. Linda seemed to be something of a mystic.

"I did not say that we were saints; that is our last name: Steve and Ginny Saint," Steve tried to explain.

"Yes, but you are also saints, aren't you?" Linda asked.

Steve admitted that yes, we were Christians. We were believers. And our last name was Saint. Linda brought her husband back to meet us, and as we talked, she told me several times how desperately she had been praying for saints to move into the vacant Grinnell Street house. Over twenty years later, we are still friends and stay in regular touch with them.

We spent two happy years in our Grinnell castle. We were part of the friendliest neighborhood in Richardson, Texas. Our house quickly became the neighborhood hangout, even though we had no pool and no TV. I may have been just a stay-at-home mom, an oddity in Dallas, but I sure made lots of cookies and got lots of hugs.

One little boy even started showing up to walk to school with our boys each morning. He always stood shyly by and watched as Steve and I kissed our two school-age boys good-bye. Then one morning as I kissed our boys, he stepped into line and lifted his face with his little lips puckered. He wanted to get a kiss too. This became a regular morning ritual for him.

Two years after we moved to Grinnell Street, a pilot who was with the same mission Steve's mom and dad had been part of asked Steve to help him do a survey of the need for air transportation in West Africa. The region had been hit with a severe drought, and famine was killing thousands of people.

When Steve came home from West Africa, he and his business partners talked about what he had seen.

"In a hundred years, it won't make much difference how successful our oil and gas business has been," I remember him saying. "What will matter is whether we obeyed God's will for our lives."

We had believed His will for our lives had been to move to Dallas, and when we received the request to go to West Africa on short notice, Steve's partners actually encouraged us to go. (It turned out to be providential. Oil and gas prices plummeted a year or so later. Our drastic reduction in drilling activity in the Permian Basin just before the bad news hit made our small company look very wise.)

We had our partners' blessings. All we had left to do was sell our house, prepare to put our things in storage, and get together all the supplies we would need for a family of six in Mali—in just three weeks. Steve, who was going to be in Mali for most of that time, put a For Sale by Owner sign in the front yard, and we got a call right away. The caller was willing to pay full price.

I had no idea what our new home would be like, but I knew it would be near the "end of the earth," just an eighth of an inch from Timbuktu on our map—and I was all right with that. I was starting to get the hang of this living by faith stuff. I had learned to take baby steps of faith. Now those steps were getting bigger and bigger as God continued to prove that He cares about the affairs of our lives and that He will always intervene on our behalf to provide what we need. He doesn't always make it easy, but He always makes it possible.

I couldn't wait to see what was next! I knew there would be lots of sand in Africa, and I was sure God would provide a castle for us there, too.

+

+

CHAPTER 5

JUST IN TIME

It was the late 1970s, and I had left Ginny and Shaun at home in Willmar to attend the annual National Religious Broadcasters' Convention in Washington DC. I wanted to be at the convention that year because I was serving on the board of a Christian radio station at the time and because my stepfather was just finishing his term as the NRB president.

While I was at the conference, a discussion in one of the sessions turned to the need for a new station manager for KVMV, a small but critical radio station on the U.S.-Mexico border. Someone asked me if I would be willing to serve in that capacity.

Whoa, I thought. *Let's not go down that trail.* After my dad was killed, Mom moved us up to the capital city of Ecuador, where she ran a busy guesthouse for the World Radio Missionary Fellowship. I spent some of my formative years growing up around the Christian radio "business." We played hide-and-seek in the studio building; I was on a kids program, *Gospel*

Bells; and I ran the control board for some programs. But radio was not a natural attraction for me. And my few experiences in management made it clear I was more of an entrepreneur than a manager.

At the time, I was in the construction business with a partner in Minnesota. We had added a small lumberyard and a real estate office, sort of a small-town one-stop shop "for all your housing needs." Business-wise, it definitely would not have been a good time for me to take off for the Texas-Mexico border.

I wasn't interested in moving, selling my half of the business, or becoming a radio station manager. But I *was* interested in doing what God wanted me to do. So although I tried to steer the KVMV discussion down a different trail, I did consider the request, hoping that a better alternative would show itself soon. That did not happen.

Finally, I felt I needed to at least make a visit to KVMV to show God I was willing. But I wanted someone to go with me, someone who knew the radio business and was astute enough to figure out that I was not the right guy for that position.

I had just the man for the job. Hardy had been on staff at the large international radio station in Ecuador. I first met him when he caught me stealing carrots from his garden on the radio station grounds. Our paths had recently crossed again in DC, when I learned that Hardy had spent years at a great Christian radio station in Minneapolis—one that we listened to all the time.

I asked Hardy if he would take a few days off and visit KVMV with me, selling the idea as an adventure trip back to the Spanish-speaking world. I offered to fly the two of us down to the border in my little plane, and although Hardy was pretty old by this time, he was young at heart, so he agreed to go with me.

Hardy and I took off for South Texas in my plane. As we flew, I remembered how scared I had once been of Hardy. It probably started when he caught me sneaking carrots from his garden. Scary moments like that can mark a fellow. But I had also been afraid of Hardy for another reason. He always seemed to have a little ball of white saliva on his lips. Few adults would have noticed, but kids pick up on stuff like that. You have to be quick witted when you have to deal with things like monsters living under your bed and other life-threatening issues on a regular basis. There was no telling what those sticky white flecks that transitioned from Hardy's lower lip to his upper lip and then back when he spoke actually meant. All of us kids knew that there was a dark and mysterious story behind this phenomenon, but no one ever dared to ask.

As Hardy and I flew toward Texas, I noticed the white flecks again, and this time, I had to ask him about it. With information like this, I might just be the hero of the next class reunion.

Turns out it was just a symptom of Hardy's high blood pressure. When he got nervous, his blood pressure went up and the flecks grew proportionately. I noticed, as we flew along, that there was a large, sticky white glob on Hardy's lower lip. Flying was definitely affecting his blood pressure. I decided I'd better mention that I was going to run the right tank dry in a little while, and the engine would quit temporarily.

When you're flying at night, especially on a clear night, you can almost always see the glow of at least one or more cities. But on this night, we were flying over a part of the United States that was so desolate, there were no lights on the ground. This was mesquite and longhorn country. I told Hardy that I wanted to be sure that I'd used every drop from one tank before starting on my left tank. He said no problem, and promptly dropped off to sleep.

He did not stay that way, however, when the gas ran out and the engine went silent. Hardy sat straight up, his eyes wild. Without even glancing at me, he panicked. His sleep-blurred mind told him that if the engine had quit we were going to crash, and he did not want to be in a crashing plane.

Hardy grabbed the door handle to exit our "doomed" plane. With a wind of about a hundred miles an hour blowing against that big Cessna door, there was no way Hardy was going to get out, no matter how hard he tried. But he did not know that. As he pulled the handle, the door popped out just enough to blast the inside of the plane with cold, loud Texas air.

It only took about three or four seconds for all of this to take place—just enough time for the fuel from the new tank to fill the fuel line and reach the engine. It came to life with a roar, just as Hardy was about to bail out. In that instant, Hardy's mind went from half asleep to being hyperawake. He suddenly realized that he was trying to jump out of a perfectly good airplane thousands of feet in the air.

He let go of the door handle like it was on fire, slumped in his seat, and grabbed at his heart. I thought he was having a heart attack. Now both of our hearts were racing. I ran my tongue over my lips to see if I had a sticky white ball of my own.

Then we started to laugh. The more we laughed, the funnier it got. Hardy kept motioning at the door handle and trying to tell me how he was about to jump. But he couldn't talk; he was laughing too hard. We laughed until we saw the lights of the border in the distance ahead of us.

Hardy was sure he had almost taken a fatal step. I was feeling the same way about moving down to Texas to take on a responsibility I was not suited for. Much like the engine fired up just in time to save Hardy's life, and God's provision to Abraham arrived just in time to save Isaac's life, I desperately needed my own "just in time" provision from God.

The U.S.-Mexico border is fraught with tension. Laws governing life on either side of the border vary widely. Both Mexico and the United States closely regulate what crosses that border into each respective country. But radio signals cannot be stopped by border patrols.

Although Mexico did not allow any religious broadcasting within its borders, it allowed radio stations to broadcast English programming into the United States, so the Federal Communications Commission reciprocated by allowing U.S. stations to broadcast in Spanish into Mexico.

KVMV, a Christian station broadcasting into Mexico, was much more important than I had originally assumed. This one little station had the potential of becoming an anchor station that could grow into a large and significant network of stations along the border. My enthusiasm for the KVMV job grew, but my sense of inadequacy for the job grew right along with it. I waited for my entrepreneurial spirit to kick my desire into gear, but it didn't.

Hardy's desire did, however. He admitted to me that he had always wanted to manage a little station like this and build its music and message format into a stencil that could be copied or adapted by other fledgling stations. He had been part of the team that had been doing that very thing at KTIS in Minneapolis.

I started to see a tiny flicker of hope at the end of the dark tunnel I had felt trapped in. I knew the job at KVMV needed to be done. But I also knew I simply could not do it—unless, maybe, Hardy was willing to go with me. Hardy would know what to do, and I could implement it.

When I mentioned the idea of my accepting the challenge if he would come with me, Hardy responded enthusiastically. He quickly began to dispense with many of the obstacles I had worried might keep him from moving from Minneapolis to McAllen. The job at KTIS? He was ready to take on one more challenge before he retired. Hardy's grown daughter with Down syndrome? She was living in a home where she functioned well and had a part-time job and other responsibilities. She was finally ready for her parents to leave.

But what about my obstacles? I knew Ginny would be game. Shaun was too young to care much, and Jaime was "still in the oven." He wouldn't even know we had moved. But I also had a business that was going great. I had a partner who depended on me to handle the sales, legal matters, and other areas of the business that my personality and background were better suited to oversee. Maybe he would say no, and that would be my excuse not to go. However, when I was honest with myself, I knew that Forry would go along with the change. He was a stalwart God follower who would never stand in the way of my doing what God called me to do. The only thing I needed to do was tell him I was sure this was what I should do. Was I sure?

I had three houses that I would have to sell. Ginny and I were living in one, and I had recently built two more on speculation. One had foundation problems that plagued me. It would not be easy to sell that one. And besides the house problems, it would not be easy to leave all the family we had in Willmar.

When Hardy and I returned to Minnesota, I quickly found a farmer who had a piece of land and an old farmhouse adjoining Forry's and my development. I talked to the farmer about trading his old house and piece of land for two of my houses. He could use one to live in and the other for a rental property. He was very interested. My brother, Phil, and his wife said they would move into the farmhouse and fix it up. If the farmer agreed to take two houses and if I could rent out our house, we would be all set for the move to the land of tacos and jalapeños.

I was sure it was going to happen. I could see God's hand fitting all the pieces into place. I was excited by now, and so was Ginny. I did not feel adequately skilled for the job, but Ginny and I were both convinced that God was leading. This was a great experiment in the art of "listen and obey" faith. I waited for the farmer to call and confirm our deal.

But the farmer did not call. Finally I called him.

"Well, uh, the wife and I really like the idea of the new house and all. . . ." Something was wrong, but what could it be? He continued reluctantly, "The kids are against it. They say this is supposed to be their inheritance and all."

I couldn't believe this was happening. Selfish children might be able to keep Ma and Pa in a drafty house that had only recently had an indoor bathroom added to it, but they couldn't thwart God's plans. If God would not make self-centered heirs get out of the way, I was convinced I should—as His agent, of course. And if the farmer and his wife would not make the deal, I would find someone else who would. There are a lot of ways to skin a cat, after all.

I was working myself into a fever. I would show the farmer and his family. And I would show all the people we had told about God's sure leading that we were not quitters. I would show them that we weren't mistaken regarding God's plan. Suddenly, I caught myself. I was starting to sound like the Humanist Manifesto: If God will not save us, we must save ourselves. Worse, I was trying to "save" God from people and circumstances that were conspiring to thwart His obvious plan. No other alternative made sense to me—until I started to listen again.

It finally occurred to me that maybe God did not need me down at KVMV after all.

But who will do what they called me to do? I asked Him. Then I remembered how ill suited I had felt for that job when they first asked me to do it. To be perfectly honest, I still couldn't see myself in that role.

If I can't do the job, who will, at this late date? Of course, the answer was Hardy! Hardy had the background and the experience. He had the vision for building what the board wanted KVMV to be. The only thing he wouldn't have if I did not go was me.

On a very small scale and, of course, a much less significant scale, this was like what God did with Abraham. He told Abraham to sacrifice the son God Himself had given Abraham. It looked like God was contradicting Himself. Why kill Isaac when he was the miracle son through whom God had promised to make Abraham a great nation? We now know that God obviously never intended for Isaac to actually be sacrificed. He just wanted to be sure Abraham was willing.

I talked with Ginny about the new development, and we both had to admit that maybe God had never intended for us to move to McAllen, Texas.

"But why did we feel His call to go?" Ginny asked.

"Maybe He just wanted Hardy to go," I said.

"Then why didn't He just call Hardy?"

I thought about it for a minute and then realized that maybe *we* were God's way of calling Hardy and Lois. When I had first told Hardy about being asked to go to KVMV, I was desperate for some help figuring out how to do what needed to be done. Ordinarily, the more uncertain an undertaking, the better I function. But this time the juices had never started flowing. My only impulse to go had been a sheer desire to be obedient to God. But my interest and my need for an expert were what had gotten Hardy interested.

My need to visit the station had also given Hardy a reason to go. I thought he had just been there as my consultant. But maybe the "Plan" was for me to be Hardy's consultant. I knew I would have to talk to Hardy and Lois about this new possibility.

"Hardy, I haven't been able to sell my properties," I started out. "But I'm confident I can sell them. What I'm not so sure about is whether I *should* sell them." No sticky white fleck yet.

"I suspect that you and you alone are God's solution for the need at KVMV. I think Ginny and I were just God's means to this end. If you go, there is no need for us to go."

It seemed so clear now: God had just been using us. But then, that is exactly what Ginny and I always prayed for. *God, You really had me fooled there for a while!*

The old farmer died. His house was bulldozed, and his field is now a park. Hardy turned out to be the perfect man for the job at KVMV. Under his leadership, the station grew into a network that now includes sixteen radio stations and repeaters stretching from the Gulf of Mexico to the Pacific Ocean.

I can still remember how confusing those days were when God seemed to be sending mixed signals to us. In hindsight, I'm quite sure that God never intended for Ginny and me to manage a radio station. We needed to be willing to go, but God had another provision that He revealed to us just in time. Some of life's sand castles are obvious. Others, like this one, are just faint outlines along the shore.

Ginny and I did move to Texas a few years later, to a house on Grinnell Street.

CHAPTER 6

BUSINESS AS UN-USUAL

I felt a little shock of excitement as I saw the car pull into our parking lot. I was sitting in my office in the lower level of our new split-level model home. My eyes were right at bumper level, so I couldn't see what kind of car it was until it pulled into the parking space right in front of my window. My excitement began to wane when I saw that the muffler was dragging almost to the ground.

When the two occupants emerged from the car, I lost what little excitement was left. Because of my unusual vantage point, my first impressions of these potential home buyers were made based on their legs and the lower half of their car. The driver was wearing tennis shoes and blue jeans. I couldn't see the label, but I knew these were no designer jeans. I'll admit that it seems a little harsh to judge someone's financial status by his or her shoes and pants, but even in normal times, I had never sold a house to someone dressed in old tennis shoes and raggy denims—and these were anything but normal times.

It was May 1981. Interest rates were at 15 percent for home loans and heading higher. Even people who arrived in luxury cars and wearing dress shoes and expensive slacks couldn't get loans to buy houses from us. And the few who could didn't want to at 15 percent interest rates.

When the passenger stepped out, I knew it was a "no sale." She lifted her feet and swiveled on the seat like older folks do. She then planted her feet in preparation for the effort of standing up. I noticed she was wearing nylons that were rolled down into a donut just below her knees. Having grown up in South America, I had seen that done many times. Down there, it was the custom of older women in the lower (poorer) classes. I didn't know what it meant in the Midwest, USA, but I assumed it meant that my chances of selling a house to this pair were not favorable.

As I headed for the front door to greet my "prospective home buyers," discouragement came over me like a cloud. It wasn't just that these people were obviously not capable buyers, but just that morning, in desperation, I had prayed and pleaded with God to show me that He was still in control and that He could bless us in spite of the lousy economy, if He chose to do so. I had specifically prayed that God would send me a customer who was ready, willing, and able to contract us to build a new house. I had even gone so far as to ask that by noon I would have a signed contract. I knew that one contract was not going to make much of a difference. But I wasn't asking to prosper while everyone else suffered. I just wanted reassurance that God was aware of what was happening to our business and that He was still able to change our fortunes if He chose to.

I had sort of a deal going with God. It seems rather arrogant of me as I look back, but I had always figured that if I did what God wanted me to do for Him, then He'd do what I wanted Him to do for me. At the time, I would have expressed it in more spiritual terms, but that was the idea.

What I had done for God was to leave the land development and construction business that I co-owned in order to work in Ecuador for four months. There, I helped supervise a large group of volunteers in building a hydroelectric dam high in the Andes Mountains.

It had all started in December, a year and a half earlier. Ginny and I took our four children to Ecuador for a visit. We hadn't been back since we were married there. Accompanying us were Ginny's sister and her husband, who owned and operated a large family farm, and a mutual friend whose family owned a large road construction company.

As we traveled around Ecuador, we saw the beginnings of the hydroelectric project that would eventually supply power for the transmitters of the World Radio Missionary Fellowship in Quito. Both my brother-in-law and our friend decided they wanted to get involved with the project. When we returned to Minnesota, they began to recruit equipment, supplies, and volunteers to help build a dam in the Andes.

I first learned of the magnitude of their efforts when I got a long-distance call from the head of engineering at WRMF in Ecuador. He wanted to verify that I was planning to accompany the large group of volunteers "I" had recruited. He said he would like me to stay for six months to a year to serve as construction coordinator because none of the volunteers spoke

Spanish or had construction experience in third world countries like I did.

My initial reaction was to say no. I couldn't leave our business for that length of time. We had employees who counted on us for work. The economy was going sour, making contracts for new houses more difficult to find. Besides all that, we were just coming into the winter season, and I needed to line up work for the spring. When the ground thawed in April, we'd have to have work lined up for the summer or we'd be hurting next winter.

I said I'd have to ask my business partner and pray about it. I wasn't sure what praying would reveal, but I was quite sure that my partner, Forry, would agree that it was impractical for me to go. I figured I could use that as an excuse to decline the offer. When I explained the situation to him, Forry did mention that the timing seemed bad, but he also recognized the opportunity for doing something of eternal significance. His response was simple: "If God is calling you to go—go. God will take care of the business."

And so we had gone, and in the end, we were pleased that we had. Working under harsh conditions near the Continental Divide, that small army of volunteers did wonders. In four months they took the hydro project from three months behind schedule to almost three months ahead of schedule. It was an amazing time.

But when we got back to Minnesota, things looked pretty bleak. I knew what some of our employees were thinking: *Sure is nice that the boss can run off and do volunteer work for God— but we're the ones who'll pay. He volunteers to be a missionary and now we go hungry.*

So here I was, asking God to remind me that He was in control of the circumstances facing our company. As soon as I prayed for a signed contract by noon, I regretted it. I wanted a sign, but I had asked for a miracle. I thought about amending the request to allow time for "processing my petition," but I didn't because I knew the compromise would make me doubt the answer. So I stuck with the noon deadline. I honestly didn't think God would pull such big strings for such a little reason, but I did expect to have until noon to find out. Now, at a quarter to ten, I already had my answer. Even if God did bring the miracle buyer to me, I'd be tied up with a teenager and her poor, old grandmother.

When I got the two ladies seated, they acted very shy. Finally the older woman looked at the younger and said, "*Preguntele que tipo de casas construyen,*"—"Ask him what kind of houses they build." As soon as I heard her question, I answered her in Spanish, "We build any kind of house you want." For a moment I forgot about my dilemma. I didn't get much opportunity to speak Spanish in Scandinavian central Minnesota, and it was clear that this woman never expected to hear it spoken by a blond-haired young gringo.

Her relief and pleasure were obvious. She explained to me as fast as her Latin tongue would allow that she hoped to get a subsidized government loan to build a house. We seldom built small houses because they were hard to do profitably. We especially shied away from government-financed projects because of the incredible red tape and the unreasonable lead time it usually took to get them approved. I doubted if this migrant family could get approval for any loan, but even if they could, I knew it wouldn't happen by noon.

Because of the language obstacle they faced, I offered to call the Farmers Home Administration to find out what "Grandma" should do to start the process. She looked at house plans while I made the call. It was almost 10:30.

It took me five minutes to get through the operator to one of the FmHA loan officers. I began to explain why I was calling when the officer cut me off.

"Who is it you're calling for?" she demanded.

"Well, it's a migrant family," I began to explain.

"Are they Spanish?" she demanded again. I could read the script from here on. I knew Grandma had probably already been to several other construction companies. I figured every contractor in Kandiyohi County had been calling FmHA about this deal, and they were tired of all the requests.

But rather than the "we're not interested" that I expected, the loan officer almost sounded excited.

"Is she still there?" she asked. I wondered if Grandma was a fugitive.

"Does she like any of your plans?" I was getting confused.

"Can you bring her over here right away?" Now I was suspicious.

What I was hearing was as likely to happen as my wife asking our kids to track mud into the house, slurp their food, and draw on the living room walls with their crayons. I asked for an explanation from the loan officer.

She hastily explained that they were about to lose their funding because they had not made any loans to minorities in two years. They hadn't made any loans because they hadn't received any minority applications. African Americans and Hispanics were as plentiful in Willmar, Minnesota, as walnuts on a cherry tree. Grandma's was the first application our FmHA office had received from an honest-to-goodness minority, and they needed her more than she needed the house. They needed me because I could translate. They also needed the contract signed as soon as possible to avoid losing their funding. The only aspect of the normal modus operandi they didn't change was the truckload of forms that had to be filled out. We jumped in the car and headed over to the FmHA office to get started.

Grandma didn't have anything to lose. She was going to be buying a three-bedroom, two-bath house with a full basement for 146 dollars a month (at that time, two-bedroom apartments rented for 300 dollars a month in that area). She couldn't understand what was going on, but she knew that, for whatever reason, she had suddenly become a celebrity, and she aimed to take it the distance. By the time I finished explaining all the forms, she had negotiated funding for a concrete driveway, brick trim, a garage, and the second bathroom, all of which FmHA usually did not fund.

By the time we were done at the FmHA office I was worn out. After receiving big *abrazos* from Grandma, I headed back to my own office. I glanced down at my watch. Twelve o'clock—noon!

I couldn't believe it. I had begged God for a sign, and He had built me a sand castle right in front of my eyes.

I was elated and, honestly, surprised. I tell others that God can do anything, and I do believe that He can, but I'm regularly surprised when He does.

Now I had my sign. Even though it was pretty clear that our business would probably not survive these tough financial times, I was at least ready to go down with a smile on my face and a song in my heart.

I looked at our business in the same way that I imagine

Abraham looked at Isaac on the altar (although I'm certainly not suggesting that the magnitude was equivalent). I didn't understand God's plan, but I knew He had one. I believed that either He would bring it back to life or He would eventually reveal that there was benefit in its demise.

Fortunately, God's plan was bigger than my imagination. After Grandma, another FmHA buyer came to us. Then another, and another, and another. Not only were we keeping our construction crews busy, we were also selling lots. In addition, a small lumberyard we had started proved to be a huge help in cutting costs so that we could make a profit even on low-budget projects.

One day Forry, who was supervising construction while I managed the selling and red tape, asked me about a particular job file. When he gave me the customer's name, I couldn't remember who the person was. When I checked my files I realized why. In the two or three weeks since I had dealt with that buyer, I had sold eight more houses and started files on several more.

A few days later, I was out in our development with a soils engineer. He asked me how we could keep so busy when so many contractors were folding. I looked around the development, where Sold signs dotted numerous lots and a good number of houses were in various stages of completion. "It's not only here, either," he said. "I see your signs all over town!"

There was no reasonable answer other than that God was blessing us. I didn't think he would understand or believe my explanation, but I offered it anyway. I'm sure he thought I was putting him on until I explained that we hadn't changed our marketing or business plan in any way. It proved to be a great opportunity to demonstrate that "God exists and that he rewards those who sincerely seek him" (Hebrews 11:6). God's reward is often internal rather than material, but dollar signs are easier for skeptics to measure.

I had many opportunities to testify to God's intervention in our business over the next year. Our success and prosperity in the midst of recession was so unusual that it began to draw attention we wished it wouldn't. One day while at the FmHA office, I told the director that I really appreciated all the work we had been getting through their office and wanted to do something to show my appreciation. I explained that our company policy was never to do anything that could be misconstrued as favor buying, but asked if I could send flowers and a thank-you note.

The director looked as if she had been shot.

"No, no, please, don't send anything, especially not now," she responded. I must have looked surprised at her strong reaction.

"Haven't you heard?" she continued. "U.S. Congressman Vin Weber's office has been asked to investigate you and our office."

I hadn't heard, but I could understand why other contractors in our area would suspect foul play. Either our good fortune was a miracle, or we were doing something illegal or even inappropriate. We were eventually cleared of all suspicions, but the investigation request served as confirmation of how dramatically God had intervened.

Years later, the financial independence we gained from this period of unusual prosperity made it possible for me to go to Africa. But that is another story of the evidence of God's existence and intervention in my life. This sand castle can stand by itself!

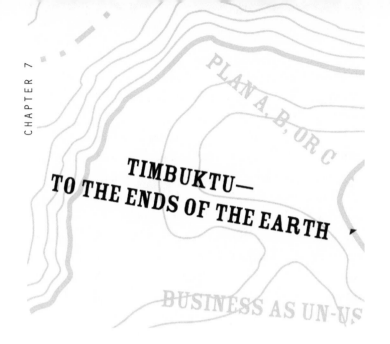

CHAPTER 7

TIMBUKTU—
TO THE ENDS OF THE EARTH

For years I thought Timbuktu was just a made-up name for "the ends of the earth." When I found out it was a real place in Africa, I developed an inexplicable fascination with it. It was in 1986 while on a fact-finding trip to West Africa for Mission Aviation Fellowship that this fascination became an irresistible urge. Timbuktu wasn't on my itinerary, but I knew I had to go there. Once I arrived, however, I realized I was in trouble.

I had hitched a ride from Bamako, Mali, five hundred miles away, on the only seat left in a Navajo six-passenger airplane chartered by UNICEF. At the time, I was told that two of their doctors were in Timbuktu and might fly back on the return flight, which meant I'd be bumped. I had decided to take the chance anyway.

Now here I was, standing by the plane on the windswept outskirts of the famous Berber outpost. There was not a spot of true green anywhere in the desolate Sahara landscape. Dust blew across the sky, blotting out the sun as I squinted in the 110-degree heat, trying to make out the mud-walled buildings of the village of twenty thousand.

The pilot approached me to report that the doctors were on their way and I'd have to find another way back to Bamako. "Try the marketplace. Someone there might have a truck. But be careful," he said. "Westerners don't last long in the desert if the truck breaks down, which happens often."

I didn't relish the thought of being stranded, but perhaps it was fitting that I should wind up like this, surrounded by the Sahara. Since I'd arrived in Africa, the strain of the harsh environment and severe suffering of the starving people had left me feeling lost in a spiritual and emotional desert.

The open-air marketplace in the center of town was crowded. Men and women wore flowing robes and turbans as protection against the sun. The men were well armed with scimitars and knives. I felt their eyes watching me suspiciously.

Suspicion was understandable in Timbuktu. Nothing and no one could be trusted there. These people had once been prosperous and self-sufficient. Now even their land had turned against them. Drought had turned rich grasslands into desert. Unrelenting sun and windstorms had nearly annihilated all animal life. People were dying by the thousands.

I went from person to person trying to find someone who spoke English, until I finally came across a local gendarme who understood my broken French.

"I need a truck," I said. "I need to go to Bamako."

Eyes widened in his shaded face. "No truck," he said, shrugging. "No road. Only sand."

By now, my presence was causing a sensation in the marketplace. I was surrounded by at least a dozen small children, jumping and pulling at me, begging for coins and souvenirs. The children grew more insistent and aggressive as their numbers increased. The situation was getting out of control. The adults ignored the pushing and the shoving that was now threatening to overwhelm me. Not only was I getting scared, I also felt terribly isolated. I tried to think calmly. *What do I do now?*

Suddenly I had a powerful desire to talk to my father. Certainly he had known what it was like to be a foreigner in a strange land. But my father was dead.

I'd felt the need to talk with my father before, especially since I'd married and become a father myself. But in recent weeks this need had become urgent. For one thing, I was new to relief work. But it was more than that. I needed Dad to help answer my new questions of faith.

In Mali, for the first time in my life, I was surrounded by people who were hostile to my faith. In a way it was a parallel to the situation Dad had faced in Ecuador. I caught myself saying the same thing Dad had wanted to say to the Indians who killed him: "My God is real. He's a personal God who cares what happens to us, and He loves you too."

And yet, especially now, as I found myself in this strange land, the question lingered in my mind: If God loves us and cares what happens to us, why did my father have to die?

All my life, people had spoken of Dad with respect: He was a man willing to die for his faith. But when they did, I couldn't help but think the murders were capricious, an accident of bad timing. Dad and his colleagues landed just as a small band of "Auca" men were in a bad mood for reasons that had nothing to do with these Americans or their faith. If Dad's plane had landed a few days later, the massacre may not have happened.

Couldn't there have been another way? It made little impact on the "Aucas" that I could see. To them it was just one more killing in a history of killings.

Thirty years later it still had an impact on me. And now, for the first time, I felt threatened because of who I was and what I believed. *God,* I found myself praying as I looked around the marketplace, *I'm in trouble here. Please keep me safe and show me a way to get back. Please reveal Yourself and Your love to me the way You did to my father.*

No bolt of lightning came from the blue, but I did have a thought. Surely there was a telecommunications office here somewhere; I could wire Bamako to send another plane. It would be costly, but I could see no other way of getting out. "Where's the telecommunications office?" I asked another gendarme. He gave me instructions in French, which I understood to mean, "Telegraph transmits only. If station in Bamako has machine on, message goes through. If not . . ." He shrugged. "No answer ever comes. You only hope message received."

Now what? The sun was marching onward across the sky. If I didn't have arrangements made by nightfall, what would happen to me? This really seemed to be the last outpost of the inhabited world. I had been told that more than a few Westerners had disappeared in the desert around Timbuktu without a trace.

Then I remembered that just before I'd started for Timbuktu, a fellow worker had told me about a famous mosque there that had been built in the 1500s. Many Islamic pilgrims visit it every year. He had also told me about a tiny Christian church near the mosque. "Look it up if you get the chance," he had said.

I asked the children, "Where is L'Église Évangélique Chrétienne?" The youngsters were willing to help, though they were obviously confused about what I was looking for. Several times elderly men and women scolded them harshly as we passed—I got the impression that they did not like the children associating with a foreigner—but they persisted. Finally we arrived, not at the church, but at the open doorway of a tiny mud-brick house. No one was home, but on the wall opposite the door was a poster showing a cross covered by wounded hands. The French subscript said, "And by His stripes we are healed."

Within minutes, a young man approached us in the dirt alleyway. The children melted back into the labyrinth of the walled alleys and compounds of Timbuktu.

The young man was handsome, with dark skin and flowing robes. But there was something inexplicably different about him. His name was Nouh Ag Infa Yatara; that much I understood. Nouh signaled he knew someone who could translate for us. He led me to a compound on the edge of town where an American missionary lived. I was glad to meet the missionary, but from the moment I'd seen Nouh I'd had the feeling that we shared something in common.

"How did you come to have faith?" I asked him through an interpreter.

The missionary translated as Nouh answered. "This compound has always had a beautiful garden. One day when I was a small boy, a friend and I decided to steal some carrots. It was a dangerous task: We'd been told that *toubabs* (white men) eat nomadic children. Despite our agility and considerable experience at stealing vegetables, the missionary caught me. But he didn't eat me; instead he gave me the carrots and some cards that had God's promises from the Bible written on them. He said if I learned them, he'd give me a Bic tick-toc."

He pulled a pen out from his robe and clicked it on and off.

So that was what the mob of children had been clamoring for! I had a couple of pens in my shirt pocket, and I'm sure that's what had triggered the mob.

"You learned them?" I asked.

"Oh, yes! Only government men and the headmaster of the school had a Bic pen! But when I showed off my pen at school, the teacher knew I must have spoken with a *toubab*, which is strictly forbidden. He severely beat me."

When Nouh's parents found out he had portions of the Christian infidels' book defiling their house, they threw him out and forbade anyone to take him in; nor was he allowed to go back to school. But something had happened. Nouh had come to believe the Bible verses he had memorized.

Nouh's mother, one of several wives, became desperate. Her own standing, as well as her children's, was in jeopardy. Finally she decided to kill Nouh. She obtained poison from a sorcerer and poisoned Nouh's food at a family feast he was allowed to attend. Nouh ate the food and wasn't affected. His brother, who unwittingly stole a morsel of meat from the deadly dish, became violently ill and remains partially paralyzed even today. Seeing God's intervention, the family and townspeople were afraid to make further attempts on Nouh's life but condemned him as an outcast.

After sitting a moment, I asked Nouh the question that only hours earlier I'd wanted to ask my father: "Is your faith so important to you that you're willing to give up everything, perhaps even your life, for it?"

Nouh nodded. "I know God loves me and I'll live with Him forever. I know it! Now I have peace where I used to be full of fear and uncertainty. Who wouldn't give up everything for this peace and security?"

"It can't have been easy for you as a teenager to take a stand that made you despised by the whole community," I said. "Where did your courage come from?"

"The missionary couldn't take me in without putting my life in jeopardy. So he gave me some books in French about other Christians who had suffered for their faith. My favorite was about five young men who willingly risked their lives to take God's Good News to Stone Age Indians in the jungles of South America." His eyes widened. "I've lived all my life in the desert. How frightening the jungle must be! The book said these men let themselves be speared to death, even though they had guns and could have killed their attackers!"

The missionary said, "I remember that story. As a matter of fact, one of those men had your last name."

"Yes," I said quietly. "The pilot was my father."

"Your father?" Nouh cried. "The story is true!"

"Yes," I said, "it's true." The missionary and Nouh and I talked for a long time. When they accompanied me back to the airfield that afternoon, we found that the doctors weren't able to leave Timbuktu after all, and there was room for me on the UNICEF plane.

As Nouh and I hugged each other, it seemed incredible that God loved us so much that He'd arranged for us to walk His trail and meet "at the ends of the earth." Nouh and I had gifts for each other that no one else could give. I gave him the assurance that the story that had given him courage was true. He gave me the assurance that God had used Dad's death for good. Dad, by dying, had helped give Nouh a faith worth dying for. And Nouh, in return, had helped give Dad's faith back to me.

CHAPTER 8

PLAN A, B, OR C

TIMBUKTU—
E ENDS OF THE EARTH

"Why did the smallest *cowodi* (foreigner) not flee? Surely, fleeing, he would have lived!"

The faces of the few warriors and the handful of women had pained, expectant looks on them. *Surely they don't really want an explanation,* I thought. Even if Pete Fleming had fled from the warriors who were spearing my father and the others, I was sure the outcome would have been exactly the same.

"Fleeing, you would just have followed him and speared," I countered. The small group of Waodani reacted as one. It was clear that none of them agreed with me.

"Having never killed, you don't understand it."

I did not understand all of the ensuing lecture. But what I did understand was their explanation that killing someone at very close range takes a great deal of determination. You have to work yourself up into a rage so great that it overcomes your natural fear that things could go wrong and you, rather than your enemy, might be the one who ends up impaled by spears and hacked by machetes.

"Being furious, you spear, and *then* having speared, you become afraid," they told me in a chorus of voices. I pictured the time I had waited behind the door in my sister's dark room. I couldn't wait to scare the wits out of her. And I did. As she groped for the light switch on the opposite wall, I sprang out from hiding and grabbed her as I let out my most terrifying scream. I rendered Kathy a quivering statue of Jell-O. But my victory was very short lived.

Kathy was older and stronger than I was. Mom was also more likely to believe her version of the story. While she was still quivering with fright, my elation turned to fear. The wages of my sin against my sister were going to be close enough to death that I wasn't going to wait around. I raced to my room upstairs, where I locked the door and began to barricade it with furniture. Then I waited in abject fear for what was surely coming. The Waodani must have felt the same way.

The Waodani continued to explain the facts of violent life to me. "Having speared two and two of the foreigners, we were already afraid. The smallest foreigner already having fled to the other side of the river, why did he not flee *omaedi* (into the jungle)?"

I had watched some of these very men follow wild pigs and deer by the animals' signs. I had followed one of the men as he tracked a large but elusive tapir for most of a day. He knew what plants the tapir wanted to eat. He told me, "Here, he slept before eating again." When we lost the tapir's tracks, he would scout around in the jungle a bit and then lead me to a place where we would pick up the trail again. It was as though he could read the tapir's mind. Following a foreigner through the jungles would have been child's play by comparison. But they were telling me that they would not have followed Pete if he had just fled into the jungle because by then their rage had already turned to fear.

Why didn't he flee? I wondered. Even if he thought they would come after him, surely instinct would have powerfully urged him to get away from the brutal savagery that was befalling his friends.

"Not fleeing *omaedi*, what did he do?" I asked.

"Standing on a log on the other side of the river, he called to us, '*Bito emite ponemopa.*'"

I recognized the phrase that Jim had learned before the men left for "Operation 'Auca.'" Loosely translated, *Bito emite ponemopa* means "I like you" or "I want to be your friend."

The attacking party had apparently understood it.

"What did you do then?" I asked.

"Kimo walked over to where he was calling, spearing him right here," said one of the men, pointing to his chest. "He fell into the water and died."

———

At the University of Washington, Pete had been a philosophy major. He did not think his colitis and frequent bad headaches allowed for serious consideration of missions as a career. Besides, he realized he had a gift for teaching and was convinced that there was a serious need for more Christian witnesses on secular university campuses.

Plan A for Pete was to teach English literature at a secular university and to marry his college sweetheart, Olive Ainslie.

Jim Elliot, a friend of Pete's, visited Seattle in July of 1951. He had some radical ideas about what Christians should and should not do. Together he and Pete went to a lecture given by a British missionary who was serving in Ecuador. In the coming weeks, as he thought about what the missionary had said, Pete's plans began to radically change. But to go to Ecuador to work with the Quechua Indians in the Amazon, Pete would need to turn his back on both his plan to teach at the university and his plan to marry Olive.

Pete was convinced that God wanted him to change his plans. In a letter he wrote to Jim, he quoted Matthew 10:39: "He that findeth his life shall lose it: and he that loseth his life for my sake shall find it" (kjv). In his letter, he went on, "God, I believe, is honored when we push great promises and commands to the greatest possible extent. Ecuador has appeared in my mind as an opportunity to put God to the test."[3]

Pete probably expected Jim to be enthusiastic about his decision, but Jim wanted him to be certain: "I would certainly be glad if God persuaded you to go with me," he wrote. "[But] there are too many walls to leap over not to be fully persuaded of God's will."[4]

Finally convinced that God wanted him to pursue Plan B, Pete broke his engagement to Olive, and he and Jim planned their trip to Ecuador. Olive was devastated. She questioned Pete, but he could not be swayed.

Do things ever go as planned in life? Young people often recite from the poem "Invictus," the lines "I am the master of my fate: I am the captain of my soul." But it is unlikely that anyone who has lived to maturity still believes it. We control little of our own fate in life, and the older we get the more we realize it.

Shortly after Pete and Jim arrived in Ecuador, Jim's college flame, Betty, showed up. She had been headed for another continent, but her plans had also changed. Jim and Betty quickly picked up where they had left off romantically, leaving Pete with some serious rethinking to do. He had broken his engagement because he thought Ecuador was too primitive and rough for women, but Betty and Jim were proving that idea wrong.

It didn't take long before Pete reconnected with Olive, and soon they were once again planning to be married.

Who ever said that those who determine to do the will of God never make mistakes? On the other hand, who can say that God's will always makes sense to those willing to follow Him or to those who judge His leading after the fact? The Bible says, "Trust in the LORD with all your heart and do not lean on your own understanding. In all your ways acknowledge Him, and He will make your paths straight" (Proverbs 3:5-6, NASB). It does not say, "Trust and your ways will *seem* straight."

Pete knew that it would be impossible to live on the fringes of territory possessed by the fierce "Aucas" and not risk the possibility of contact. It was this sort of danger that had first led him to believe that he must remain single in order to serve in such a remote and dangerous setting. But Pete's thinking on this matter had obviously made an about-face. Just before returning to the States to at last marry Olive, he wrote in his journal, "I feel that if pushed to it, Olive would rather have me die after we had lived together than to indefinitely postpone our wedding in the possibility that something fatal might happen."[5]

Pete and Olive were finally married, and by September of 1954 they were headed back to Ecuador to start their life of service to the Quechuas together.

Almost exactly one year later, my dad was flying Pete and two Quechua men from northwestern Quechua territory to another Quechua village to the southeast. The flight would cross the territory of the dreaded "Aucas." Just fifteen minutes from the old Shell Oil Company airstrip, where fellow missionaries Ed and Marilou McCully were living on the edge of "Auca" territory, Pete and Dad spotted a small clearing with several houses. They knew it was an "Auca" village.

Pete wrote to a friend about what happened: "I had the thrill of seeing my first Auca houses. . . . We concluded that we ought to begin immediately making frequent visits to them dropping presents."[6]

Another major change of plans? This would be Plan C.

———

Pete could have lived. Rather than simply standing on the log and calling to his attackers, he could have fled. He could have made his way upriver, where the Quechuas would have found him. Then he could have told the rest of us exactly what had happened to our fathers and husbands and friends. He could have saved us years of wondering why the very same Waodani who had exchanged gifts with Dad and Ed during three months of weekly "bucket drops" suddenly turned and killed them without any warning.

It is dangerous to second-guess God. I hesitate to do it, but the alternative here is to miss an incredible lesson. Does God actually have an interest in our daily decisions? Does He care what we do and how we do it? Does He really have a specific plan for our lives that we can discover? Or is He distant and mute, unknowing and uncaring?

Pete had been confident that God wanted him to teach at the University of Washington, where he could spiritually influence secular students in his own backyard. There, he would not have to find them or win their confidence; they would come to him. He would have had a natural relationship with them as their professor.

Plan B seemed to abandon Pete's obvious intellectual bent and his gift of teaching and would require a physical hardiness that he did not have. At first, at least, it also required that he dramatically break his commitment to marry Olive Ainslie. It would have been difficult, from a purely practical standpoint, to make sense of Plan B, except perhaps that it was more likely that someone would fill his place at the university than in the jungles of Ecuador.

But leaving the practical side out of the equation, Pete—who had been sure of God's leading to teach at the University of Washington—was just as sure of God's leading to Ecuador. Those who don't believe in God's specific leading or who have never submitted themselves to it might find it difficult to see how two such radically different paths could really be God's plan. But, knowing Pete's serious intellectual nature, I'm certain that he wasn't just imagining God's leading.

If that wasn't perplexing enough, Pete radically changed courses one more time, putting his life and ministry—as well as the future of his new wife—in jeopardy. With Plan C, he believed with all his heart that God led him to accept a role in Operation "Auca," even though it ended with his standing on a log, calling to the ruthless warriors who were killing his friends, instead of following every natural instinct and fleeing from them.

Is it possible to make sense of so many major course changes in such a short period of time? How can we ever justify the tragedy that needlessly ended it all? We can, if we believe that God had a plan.

I won't be so arrogant as to suggest that I can tell, even from this later vantage point, exactly what God had in mind for Pete and Olive. But that does not preclude us from drawing limited conclusions about God's intentions as the results of those historic actions become evident.

+

For fifty years, I have unintentionally served as verification that the story of the five Ecuadorean martyrs is true. Total strangers come up to me all the time in church, at camp, even in Wal-Mart, to ask if I am Steve Saint, son of the martyr Nate Saint. This has happened thousands of times—no, it has to be tens of thousands of times by now.

When I acknowledge that I am Nate's son, they invariably describe for me the impact this story has had on their lives. I have been to some pretty unusual places—Haiti, the Dominican Republic, Mexico, Guatemala, Costa Rica, El Salvador, Panama, Belize, Colombia, Ecuador, Peru, Canada, England, France, Belgium, Netherlands, Switzerland, Austria, Germany, Czechoslovakia (before the split), Russia, India, Sri Lanka, Afghanistan, Cuba, Nigeria, Senegal, and even Timbuktu in Mali, West Africa—and everywhere I've gone, people have told me how they have been encouraged to live for their faith by these five men who were willing to die for theirs.

I have never tried to keep track of all the stories that have been relayed to me, but most of them share a common theme: "It was worth it for *me*; the price you paid is paying dividends in my life and through my life to the lives of others."

Pete was the last of the five men to commit to being part of the contact party. He was the least likely candidate for jungle service. Why was he the one left calling on the log when he could have fled and lived? I don't know. I do have a feeling about it, however. It's an idea that came to me when the men who speared Pete and the others were finally able to share the details of the killings with me. They said they did not understand why the men reacted as they did.

"Why, not shooting us, did they just die? Why did the one who had not been speared just stand there and call to us when he could have fled and lived?"

Listening to their description of the event, I found myself trying to find a providential explanation for Pete's death, and it occurred to me that if any one of the men had lived to tell what had happened, the world's reaction to the story would have probably been very, very different.

I can believe that everything that happened was just the luck of the draw, merely the result of time and chance. Or I can believe that even the smallest circumstances of our lives are part of an intricately detailed plan laid out before time began. It takes a leap of faith either way. What tips the scales for me are the growing numbers of God signs I have seen along life's trail.

This story would not have been "this story" if Pete had stayed with Plan A or even Plan B. Even though Plan C ended in his own death, Pete was willing to follow that path because he trusted God's leading completely.

God wrote His story, using the lives of these five men and their families, as a sand castle for people far beyond Waodani territory, beyond Ecuador, and even beyond South America.

Pete changed his plans. I don't think God did. I suspect this was what He had planned all along.

CHAPTER 9

WIDOWS' STORIES

The old man was in excruciating pain. For days he had been burned and frozen and had sharp objects jabbed under his fingernails. He was stretched on a rack, and his arms and legs were pulled out of joint. He was starved, not only for food but also for sleep. His throat was so dry that he could hardly have croaked out the confession his tormentors were so determined to get from him.

Finally, almost out of his mind from the incessant torture, the man said, "Stop. Oh, please stop, and I will confess and recant." He simply could not take the pain any longer.

"No!" called one of the beautiful young women who had been forced to watch the gruesome torture. "How can you, who have witnessed so much of God's mercy and intervention on your behalf, now deny Him this close to the end of your natural life? Oh, go on and serve Him just a few minutes longer and then enter into your reward forever."

The old man, still attached to the terrible torture machine, glanced at the young woman. He was her elder. She had learned to trust God under his teaching. Her words cut through his conscience like a knife. Suddenly, the full realization of what he was doing hit him. To avoid the pain, he had agreed to deny his faith and relationship with the Savior who had so willingly suffered and died for him. But he could not quit believing.

The torture chamber was suddenly rent by the sounds of an agony beyond anything those cold stone walls had heard before.

"Oh God who has not withheld any good thing from me, forgive me now for offering to deny Thee even for a minute of time. Grant me now Your grace to feel the pain You felt for me, and then receive me into Your presence."

The torturers, at first, would not let the old man take back his decision to recant. But he begged them to begin their dastardly deeds again. And he began to encourage the members of his congregation, who would soon undergo what was being done to him, to stand firm. His torturers could not overlook this. They mercilessly went back to work, inflicting the worst pains imaginable on the old man's body. Even as they did, he looked at the young woman who had stepped forward to give him strength when his flagged. She understood the look in his eyes and the soundless words formed on his lips.

After the old man expired, the young woman was stripped naked and raped in front of her family and friends; she suffered even worse torture than the old man had been forced to undergo. Her beautiful body was unrecognizable long before life mercifully relinquished what was left. The old man was eighty. She was sixteen.

This is how I remember a story in *Fox's Book of Martyrs*. I was about the age of the young girl in the story when I read it, and I wondered how I would react if I was asked to deny my faith under threat of being tortured to death. Being the son of a martyr, I guess it is natural that I would try to imagine my response to what they had to face.

When I was young, I often caught myself daydreaming about making an impossible basket in a critical ball game to win a tournament just as the buzzer sounded. Sometimes I imagined during a football game leaping into the air to intercept a pass and then running it back for a touchdown as everyone watched in amazement. But those dreams died out as I matured and found my own place in life. As we age, we come to grips with the sobering fact that most of us are just common, ordinary people whose lives will never make headlines and whose deeds will never be recorded in history books.

It was only after reaching fifty years of age that I became fully aware of the heroic details in the lives of five women— details that forced me to wonder how my character and faith measured up to theirs. These women were not strangers. One of them, in fact, was my own mother. They were the widows whose husbands had been brutally speared to death in South America. Newspaper and magazine articles and a number of books have been written about their husbands. Plays have been written and performed about them. But these women have been known simply as "the wives of the five missionary martyrs, you know, from 1956."

I thought I knew these women's stories. They were my mom's best friends. I stayed in their homes, their children were my friends, and our common background dictated that we would stay in close touch for decades. But it wasn't until I was asked to help make a documentary film and a movie that I realized how much more there was to the story that inextricably linked our lives together.

The director of the dramatic documentary *Beyond the Gates of Splendor* asked me to interview the widows because I knew the minute details of their husbands' deaths. He wanted them to feel comfortable discussing very personal details about this traumatic event in their lives and the drastic changes the highly publicized deaths of their husbands set in motion.

Each interview I conducted with these five women was unique because their personalities were unique. But there were several questions that I knew I had to ask all of them if their interviews were going to really connect with the documentary's audience. One of those questions was, "Do you remember the last time you saw your husband?" Another one was, "What was going through your mind as you and your husband weighed the risk and return involved in attempting contact with the most violent tribe of people on planet Earth?"

My first interview was with Aunt Betty (Elisabeth Elliot). After we had talked for a while, I asked if she remembered the last time she saw her husband Jim.

"Yes," she told me. "We were at our house in Shandia when we heard your dad's plane land down at the airstrip. Jim stood up immediately, grabbed his backpack, and headed for the door. He was so excited that he didn't even say anything; he just got up and headed for the door. I jumped up to follow and was right there behind him. But before I got to the screen door, it slammed shut, and he had already started down the trail to the airstrip."

As she spoke, Aunt Betty had a slight look of hurt on her face as she recounted events that had taken place fifty years earlier.

"As I watched Jim walk down that path, I thought to myself, *Chances are I'll never see him again.*" She followed down the path to the little jungle airstrip behind her strong, handsome, and intelligent husband of two years.

I was intrigued with the life drama Aunt Betty was opening up to me. I did not want to interrupt the very personal story of what I knew to be her last interaction with the man she loved, so I waited for her to go on. As I waited, I could almost see her standing on the edge of the airstrip: tall, intellectual, vulnerable. I had spent some time in Shandia after Uncle Jim was killed. I knew the house, the path, and the little airstrip that ended in a cliff that fell away to the jungle river far below. In my mind's eye, I could clearly picture the unusual view overlooking the Amazon rain forest along the Andes Mountains.

I waited, but Aunt Betty did not go on. In the awkward instant when two people are both waiting for the other to say something, I realized that Aunt Betty was allowing me a unique look into the mysterious inner workings of the human soul. This woman I had known all my life, a woman who had fears, insecurities, and dreams just like I did, had come to a pivotal point in her life that day her husband walked out the door. She knew that when he got into that little yellow plane with my dad and disappeared over the green canopy to the east, her hopes for the future might be drastically altered forever. And yet she did not make any attempt to stop what was happening. She did not plead with her young husband. She did not ask my dad for last reassurances. She did not even cry out to God to intervene.

I could tell Aunt Betty had nothing else to say about this dramatic last contact with her husband. Her silence told me she was finished. My own silence was involuntary. I had ceased to be a "nephew," interviewer, or member of the film crew. I was once again a teenager, reading *Fox's Book of Martyrs* and wondering if I could ever measure up to the kind of faith that had just been revealed to me in the life of this woman.

———

When I asked Pete Fleming's widow, Olive, the same question, she told me that before the men were martyred, she had had a dream in which she saw her husband's body—along with those of my dad and their three companions—floating lifelessly in the river by the little sandbar Dad was going to use as a landing strip. It seemed to me that she hadn't simply been concerned about the possibility of danger; she had actually had a premonition of what was about to happen.

Olive had been jilted at age twenty, when Pete thought God was calling him to Ecuador as a single man. At age twenty-two she accepted Pete's change of heart and traded the only life she knew for the potpourri of Ecuadorean cultures and languages.

During her first year in Ecuador, Olive got pregnant twice and miscarried both times—alone, since Pete was frequently away from home. She was studying Spanish, the national language of Ecuador. The plan was for her to learn Spanish first and then start learning Quechua. Once she mastered both languages, she would join Jim and Betty Elliot, Ed and Marilou McCully, and Pete to work among the jungle descendents of the Incas.

After such a traumatic year, Pete was understandably reluctant to join my dad, Jim, Ed, and a missionary friend of Dad's from the south jungle, Roger Youderian, in their high-risk venture to reach a notoriously violent Amazon tribe. But at the last minute, he finally decided to be the fifth member of Operation "Auca."

Surely, I thought, *it would not have been difficult for Olive to talk Pete into sitting this little "side adventure" out. It would have been perfectly reasonable for her to want to keep Pete home, under the circumstances.*

"Do you remember the last time you saw Pete?" I asked.

Olive responded immediately. "I remember it vividly," she said. She explained how Pete had arranged for her to fly to be with my mother in the little oil company town of Shell Mera, about thirty air miles away on the edge of the jungle.

"I got into the plane with Johnny (the other missionary pilot). I looked through the open door at Pete, and I was sure I would never see him again."

This time, I felt the need to prompt Olive to go on: "What happened then?" I asked.

Olive turned to me and stated matter-of-factly, "So I flew to Shell to be with your mother."

Once again, I was stunned. Here was a twenty-three-year-old woman in a foreign country, living in a strange culture and surrounded by people she could not communicate with, saying good-bye to the man she had been married to for just one short, painful year. In her vivid dream, she had already seen his lifeless body floating in a silt-laden little river in the middle of the jungles. Yet she did not even attempt to change what was about to happen.

I was sitting in Olive's own living room. I had known her all of my life, but suddenly I saw her as a total stranger. Something was drastically wrong with what she was telling me. A young woman doesn't just say good-bye to her husband when she knows he is going off to die. Was it possible that she simply didn't love him? No, she waited for him for years, and they had only just been married. Maybe her dream hadn't been as real as I took it to be. But I had seen the pain in her eyes when she told me about it. I could tell she could still recall images from that dream five decades later. Yes, the dream was real, and it was still vivid in her mind.

There was only one explanation for the calm acceptance of the terrible tragedy that was about to befall young and innocent Olive Ainslie Fleming. She trusted God.

As we talked that day, I realized that I am only eighteen years her junior. At seventy years of age, she is now married to a retired professor; she's also the mother of three and grandmother of a growing group of grandchildren. She is vivacious to the point of being bubbly at times. She interacts with family and neighbors and still likes to snow ski. And yet, under the deep disguise of normalcy is hidden a faith that took my breath away when I saw her true character.

As these realizations struck me, I just could not go on with the interview. The question that filled my mind was not one for her to answer. It was a question for me. Where does an ordinary person find an extraordinary faith such as this?

When I was interviewing Marilou McCully, I felt somewhat ill at ease. Her three sons had been my friends when we were growing up. Marilou and her three boys stayed in Ecuador after her husband and their dad was killed, along with my own. They lived just down the block, where Aunt Marilou ran a boarding house for children from other parts of Ecuador who attended an English-speaking school in Quito.

The McCully dorm was the most fun place in the world when we were in grade school. I was in awe of my friends' mother. She could play the piano beautifully, but I knew that wasn't the reason men regularly tried to interest her in remarrying. She was talented, fun, efficient, and very handsome. I could tell that even in grade school.

She never remarried, though. I never understood why until we were gathering old pictures and movie footage for *Beyond the Gates*. I came across several movie clips that showed Marilou with Ed, along with friends and family. You would have to be stone-cold dead not to notice how Marilou watched Ed's every move. It was obvious that their marriage was special.

Marilou told me that she wasn't planning to get married when she met Ed.

"But he made me want to," she said. No one after that could make her want to. She was a one-man woman.

As Aunt Marilou was describing Operation "Auca" to me, her eyes twinkled with excitement, even though she was telling me about things that had happened long ago. She talked as though recalling exciting events that had just taken place rather than remembering details of a terrible and tragic ordeal half a century old.

As we worked our way up to that fateful day when the only man this woman had ever loved was brutally speared and hacked to death, she kept telling me how excited they were. And as she spoke, Marilou repeated over and over: "We were so sure of God's leading and protection."

Every time she said it, I felt uncomfortable because I knew where this story was going, and it was far from what I would refer to as protected. We were working our way inexorably toward the point in the story where some Quechua friends of Ed's delivered one of his shoes and his watch to the search party. Ed's Indian friends had gone ahead of the search party, risking their lives to find out what had happened to their mentor and friend, *Eduardo*. They found his body riddled with spears and badly hacked by machetes.

Ed's body had washed farther downriver than the other four bodies. The Quechuas told the search party that Ed's body was too far downriver to return it to the beach where the five *missioneros* had made such a promising first contact with the "Aucas" just two days before they were massacred. I don't think that was the reason. I think they could not bring themselves to handle the tattered and torn remains of the friendly, fun-loving *missionero* they had come to love and respect.

But they also loved his wife, *Madi-luu*. They knew that she would not rest easy unless she had incontrovertible evidence that they had found Ed and knew that he was dead. So they removed one of his shoes from his body. No one else in the jungle had shoes as large as *Don Eduardo*. They also brought back his wristwatch, thinking, no doubt, that Marilou would recognize it.

Even though they had chosen to live on the more dangerous side of the river, Marilou and Ed had been sure that God was leading them and protecting them in what otherwise would have been a dangerous undertaking. Ed had built on that side of the river because he wanted to be near the Shell Oil Company airstrip, and he was hoping that living there might eventually lead to a friendly contact with the "Aucas." Marilou had two young boys and was eight months pregnant with a third. She was living inside the territory of a tribe whose very name meant "naked savages" in the Quechua language. And still, she felt safe and secure.

I have been ambushed by an interviewer on more than one occasion. I was determined to make my interviews with the five widows real, but these were women I knew, loved, and respected. I could not ambush them or surprise them into saying something they really did not want to share. But Marilou almost seemed to be setting *me* up by repeatedly telling me how safe she and Ed felt about attempting face-to-face contact with the "Aucas." I knew I would have to ask Marilou this obvious but painful question, so I plunged right in: "When the search party handed you Ed's shoe and his wristwatch, what did you think about God's leading and protection then?"

This still talented, perky, and beautiful woman of almost eighty looked surprised and a little perplexed. I just hoped she would realize that she, not I, had set up this unavoidable question. I knew there could only be two obvious explanations for what had happened to Ed. Either God hadn't led, or He hadn't protected. Otherwise Ed would not have been killed, right? But he was killed. Or maybe God had been leading *and* protecting, but the situation had just gotten out of control. Could God have been sleeping or distracted?

I waited for Marilou's answer. I waited for the dark cloud to take the sparkle out of her eye. But it didn't happen. For just a second she looked confused. Then she looked back at me with the same enthusiastic intensity that had taken over as she had told me of events leading up to this point. And she gave me her answer: "I was *still* sure of His leading and protection."

I still choke up with emotion when I remember that interview that took place outside of Seattle with Mount Rainier as our backdrop. Only a miracle of faith could explain what I had just been told. It had to be that, or lunacy. But Marilou McCully was no lunatic. No, she was a hero of the faith. How could I have known her so well for so long without fully realizing this?

When the Bearing Fruit film crew came to ask my permission to make *Beyond the Gates of Splendor*, I insisted that they ask the Waodani first. At the time, I thought that would be the end of their pursuit. But they were so passionate about making this story into a broad-audience film that they agreed to my condition. After we had been into Waodani territory and then returned to Shell Mera on the edge of the jungle, I heard that Barbara Youderian was temporarily back in Ecuador, where she had continued to work after Roger's death. She had retired to the United States but had come back to Ecuador to help in a youth camp near Shell.

I was impressed with the film team and wanted them to have the pleasure of meeting one of the principal players in this story, so I borrowed a vehicle and drove them a few miles up the road from Shell to the camp where Barbara was working. When I finally located the rustic stilt house where Barbara was staying, there were no lights on. Even though it was only about eight o'clock, I knew that jungle people go to bed early, so I knocked on the screen door. I was just about to give up when I heard a sleepy voice call out, "Who is it?" I recognized Barbara's voice.

"It's Steve Saint, Aunt Barb," I called out.

"Oh, dear me," she said, "I'm not dressed for company." But she came to the door anyway, pulling her robe around her and inviting me in. I was a little embarrassed, but I had a whole van full of men who couldn't wait to meet one of the actual women in this story they loved so much, so I knew I had to press on. "Actually, Aunt Barb, I've got some friends with me who really want to meet you. We've just come out of the jungle, and we're all jungly and stinky, so you don't have to be embarrassed about how you are dressed. We'll only stay for a few minutes if you don't mind me bringing them in."

She agreed, and I brought in the troops. She offered to make coffee, but the men were so mesmerized by meeting the "real Barbara Youderian" that they didn't want to waste any of her precious time having her make coffee.

Barbara was a little embarrassed, entertaining strangers so "late," in her nightgown. I carried the conversation for a while, telling Barbara about our flight into Tiwaeno, our hike into the next river valley, and our dugout canoe trip down the Ewenguno River to Nemompade. I explained that I wanted the film crew to really understand what it was like to live in the jungle. You can't understand that without walking a jungle trail or spending at least a few hours in a hand-hewn dugout canoe. Once we were in Nemompade, where Ginny and I had our jungle home, we put everyone up in hammocks, and the Waodani generously shared their manioc, plantains, and jungle meat.

Barbara was a good sport and listened attentively, but I could tell she was tired, so after about ten minutes, I started wrapping up our visit. That is when film producer Tom Newman joined in the conversation. In hindsight, I think everyone wanted to ask Barbara questions but didn't want to intrude any further on her privacy. Tom did not want to assert himself until he realized that this might be his only opportunity.

He told Barbara that just after he came to faith in Christ, he was desperate to learn about the lives of contemporary people of faith. One of the first books he read was the book from which the new documentary would take its name. *Through Gates of Splendor* had first been a condensed book my stepdad, Abe VanDerPuy, wrote for *Reader's Digest.* Then Elisabeth Elliot used the same title for the book she wrote based on the five martyrs' journals and the five widows' letters and recollections.

Tom explained how this story had deeply affected his life and how this had always been the story he had most wanted to make into a movie. It was obvious that he knew the story well. It was also obvious that he had something on his mind. When he realized we were about to leave, he asked Barbara if he could ask her just one question—something he had wanted to know for years.

Barbara blinked a few times, apparently surprised that anyone would have wanted to ask her a question for such a long period of time. She said she would be happy to answer his question if she knew the answer.

"You were living way out in the jungles with Roger and your two young children," Tom began. "Then Nate asked Roger to help build the mission hospital in Shell. There he met Ed, Pete, and Jim. The next thing you knew, Nate had asked Roger to be a member of the Operation 'Auca' contact team. Your lives were suddenly changed as preparations were made for the face-to-face contact. I know you moved to Arajuno to be with Marilou during Operation 'Auca.'"

Tom was telling the story instead of asking a question, but I was impressed with how much he knew. I could tell Barbara was also surprised by how much he had obviously read about her life and the circumstances leading up to the deaths of the five men.

"So here you are," Tom continued. "You went to Ecuador to serve God. You lived with people who took shrunken heads. Roger left to help build a hospital where sick jungle Indians could be cared for, and then he joined Operation 'Auca.' A few days later you learn that Roger has been speared to death. He is never coming home, and your entire world has been turned upside down."

We were all sitting there trying to imagine the agony, upheaval, and uncertainty that Barbara must have gone through in those dark and difficult days. Tom had us on the edge of our seats both physically and emotionally when he finally asked his question.

"What I badly want to know is this: When you asked God why, what did He tell you?"

Barbara looked perplexed for a minute. I could tell that a few of the men thought maybe she had been offended by Tom's very personal question. But I knew that she simply did not have a pat answer. There was dead silence as the question hung in our minds, waiting for an answer from this sweet, aging, and unassuming missionary pioneer.

After what seemed like a very long pause to formulate her answer, Barbara cleared her throat and answered. "Well, I guess it just never occurred to me to ask God why."

I have never heard a simpler or more eloquent statement of faith. After sitting quietly for a few minutes, I thanked Barbara for allowing us to visit, and we left. There was very little conversation during our ride back down the road to Shell Mera. We all knew we had just heard a profound example of faith.

───────

Too much of a good thing is not a good thing. When I began to interview the fifth widow, my own mother, we ran into a problem.

The advantage of having me conduct interviews for *Beyond*

the Gates of Splendor was that I knew the details of the film's story. When one of interviewees passed by a vignette of significant interest, I could tell that we had just missed a small treasure and could take us back to pick it up. The strategy worked so smoothly that the interviews usually became animated personal discussions between old friends, whether the interviewee was a Waodani warrior, a soldier, or a widow. With my mother, however, the interview took on the shorthand nature that characterizes an inside joke. As she answered my questions, she would often say, "Well, as you know, Steve . . ."

Yes, I knew, but the audience didn't. Finally, after several unsuccessful attempts to get our interview on a sound footing, the film's director took my place as my mother's interviewer.

My own opportunity to interview Mom and to be as deeply and personally affected by her faith as I had by the other four widows' came after *Beyond the Gates* was released and just before *End of the Spear* was finished.

Mom had been fighting cancer off and on for years. It had finally come back a fourth time, and this time it had spread throughout her body. There was no way medically to fight it off any longer, so Mom came to live out her last weeks with Ginny and me. It was a very special time for all of us. In spite of the fact that Mom had begun retaining huge amounts of fluid that had to be drained off more and more frequently and was in constant pain, she maintained her enthusiastic outlook on life.

It was impossible to slip in and out of the hospital unnoticed for Mom's frequently required procedures. Mom knew no strangers and could make friends with anyone who was still breathing. Nurses would vie to care for her, and one doctor even asked to be allowed to do her paracentesis, even when it meant he would have to commute from another hospital to do so.

But Mom was going downhill physically. On one visit we discovered that seven liters of fluid had collected, collapsing one of Mom's lungs. She had to be hospitalized for two days that time. As we drove home from the hospital, I realized that one of these days soon we would be going home without Mom, and I would have broken a promise I had made to my sister and brother.

Our family has faced death enough times that it does not hold us in terror. In fact, our family as a whole believes that death is not the end of life but merely a marker along the way. But I had promised my brother, Phil, and my sister, Kathy, that before Mom died, I would videotape her telling her life story so we could pass it on to our grandchildren.

After having seven liters of fluid drained from her abdomen, Mom was in a great deal of pain. Her sensitivity was so acute that when I hit several lane-divider reflectors on the way home from the hospital, the mild thumping of the car's wheels made her groan involuntarily.

My timing was bad, but I knew I had to film Mom immediately, or the opportunity would be lost forever. Ginny realized what I was about to do, and she gave me a look that could not be misinterpreted: This was the wrong time to ask Mom to sit up in a chair and tell her life story. I agreed.

But all the right times had already passed. The benefits of eighty years of life lessons were about to be buried along with Mom's collapsing body. When I asked Mom if we could do the interview we had mentioned and postponed for over a year, she answered, "Oh, my!"

But immediately after that involuntary response, I saw her

smile in the rearview mirror. "Sure," she said. "Let's do it. I feel fine."

I made a call to two friends, who dropped what they were doing and headed for our house with professional cameras, lights, and microphones. By the time Ginny had laboriously helped Mom change into an appropriate dress, Dianne and Evan had converted our living room into a studio. Mom sat down in a straight-backed chair and said she was ready when we were.

I remembered what had happened the last time I had interviewed Mom, so I knew I would have to take a different tactic this time. Instead of trying to steer the interview, I would simply act as Mother's audience.

My decision to merely be my mother's listener was made easier by the fact that I realized I did not know much about the part of Mom's life before I was born. Being both mother and father to three children while working as a registered nurse in a mission hospital and running a busy guesthouse was not conducive to telling us children "When I was a little girl . . ." stories.

Mom began by telling what it was like to grow up during the Depression. Her dad lost his farm in Missouri and moved the family to Idaho, where he and Grandma Farris had a small concentration of relatives. For the first time in my life, I realized how poor Mom's family had been. They were poorer than the proverbial church mice—they didn't even have a church to live in. Instead, Grandpa rented a succession of cheap houses and apartments. My mother graduated as valedictorian of her large high school class while her family lived in a garage behind a modest home in Parma, Idaho. I did not need to make myself lean forward, smile, and nod to draw out my mother's life story.

I was inexorably drawn into it. And Mom was responding to my intense interest. When she realized I was surprised about the circumstances of her life during the critically formative high school years, she filled in more detail.

"Are you telling me that you graduated as valedictorian while sleeping in a shed in the backyard of a home so modest that the owners had no car to need the shed?" I asked.

"I guess we were poor, but I never remember thinking we were. Mom and Daddy always welcomed my friends over for dinner or to spend the night. No matter how little we had, my mother could always stretch it a little further. I think those were important times for me. Years later, when Nate and I moved to Ecuador, we had to start out living in a tent on the edge of the jungles. We had no running water, no electricity, and no laundry facilities. The only thing we had much of was visitors."

Mom didn't say it, but I knew she was also pregnant with my sister, Kathy, at the time.

When the time drew near for Kathy to be born, Dad took Mom to the nearest clinic—a day's travel away in Quito, high in the Andes Mountains. While Mom was there, Dad had a major flying accident and broke his back. He had to be taken to Panama City for treatment, so Mom had her baby alone in a foreign country.

But before she got to that part, Mom had more to tell about leaving home to get her nursing degree in Southern California. She told how growing up without money helped her when she had to really stretch her pennies to get through school.

While she was there, she was amazed to find how carelessly most of the other nurse cadets lived, both financially and morally. One nursing cadet confided to Mom and a friend that she was a Christian too but did not want anyone to know. She had a personal faith in God, but she did not want it to hold her back from living like she didn't.

"Years later, she told me how sorry she was that she had denied her faith in nursing school. She married a man who had no interest in spiritual things. It was a tough marriage that never would have happened if she had been open about her faith."

Not only did Mom believe in God, she also really believed that God had a plan for her life.

"It was during nursing school that 'a real live missionary' came to our church. As soon as my friend and I got off duty, we ran all the way to the big old church we attended. The place was packed, so we ended up in the highest balcony."

I pictured a huge, round, wooden auditorium with multiple balconies reaching right up into the high rafters.

"I had been interested in missions for a long time, but I had never met a real missionary. As that missionary woman told about her life, I wondered if I could handle all the hardships she had faced." Mom stopped for a moment before continuing. "I had no idea that I would have to face a great deal more than she did. At the end of the service, they gave an invitation for anyone who was willing to give his or her life to missionary service to come forward. I ran down the circular staircase as fast as I could, all the way to the front of the auditorium. When I got there I told God, *I want Your will for my life at any cost.*"

At that point, Mom's eyes teared up and her face momentarily distorted with the memories of life pains she had suffered. She talked about how difficult it had been to bury two husbands prematurely. Then she mentioned having cancer for the fourth time. Her voice throughout the interview was husky from the pain she was suffering.

Then the sparkle came back to her eyes. She straightened up in her chair and pulled her shoulders back like the trooper she had been throughout life. "If I had it to do all over again," she commented with great resolve, "I would still say, *Lord, Your will for my life at any cost!*"

Mom's health quickly declined in the days following that interview. When we told her we needed hospice to help us, Mom was troubled. She dreaded having a stranger help in her care. Ginny and I were apprehensive too. We wanted to remain in control of her last days, but we really needed the help hospice offered. Unfortunately, we knew we couldn't choose who would come to help.

"We have to pray that God will send us just the perfect person," Mom explained to Ginny and me, so we signed the forms and steeled ourselves for the hospice nurse's first visit.

The woman who came was pleasant and professional, but we wanted someone special—someone handpicked for Mom.

The nurse told us she would need some personal information, starting with Mom's legal name. Mom had started life as a Farris. Then she became a Saint, and finally a VanDerPuy when she married our wonderful stepdad. We gave her name as Marjorie VanDerPuy.

"Where have you lived?" the nurse went on.

"Well, I spent forty years in South America and then some years in Lincoln, Nebraska, and then we moved here to Florida."

The nurse got a funny look on her face. Either something was bothering her or she was trying to remember something.

"VanDerPuy? Marjorie? You aren't Marj Saint VanDerPuy by any chance, are you?"

My mother nodded.

The nurse held her face in her hands for an instant and then blurted out, "You don't know me, but I certainly know you. Because of your story and what you did with your life, my husband and I have spent our lives as missionaries. Now here I am meeting you face-to-face!"

This had happened to Mom hundreds of times over the years, but this time was different. Mom had specifically cried out to God for one last favor. She had accepted death and tragedy with a stoic and confident faith for over sixty years. She looked on hardships and deprivation almost as blessings. But Mom just couldn't face having a stranger take charge of her last days on earth. Ginny and I had agreed, but only Mom thought to ask God to pick just the right caregiver to help us through the final stages of her dying process.

And God gave Mom what she asked for: a nurse who already loved and admired Mom, and one she could admire in return. Mom's house had always been filled with guests coming and going, people Mom befriended in her travels or people who sought Mom out for counsel because they were facing painful or difficult times. But I don't think anyone ever became part of our family more quickly than Mom's hospice angel.

I realized then that sometimes it takes more faith to ask God for important little things than it does for critical big things. It was clear what the title of Mom's last interview should be: "Your Will for My Life at Any Cost." God and Mom had an interesting partnership. He called the shots and she did His bidding. She let Him write the story and trusted Him, whatever the outcome. And He showed her that her faith was well placed—right to the very end.

———

The interviews I was privileged to do with Elisabeth, Olive, Marilou, Barbara, and Mom have marked my life. They are powerful God signs that give me courage. These days, zealots are blowing themselves up "for God" and killing people around the world in the name of faith. But what made these five women of faith stand out to me was not what they did for God but the quiet way God reached out and met their emotional and spiritual needs in times of crisis.

Sand castles are not the cathedrals we build for God but the evidences we see when God personally reaches out to remind us of His existence and His love for us. The children of Israel commemorated these events by raising piles of stones for their children and grandchildren to see and ask about. We can commemorate God signs in our lives by picking up a video recorder. Or we can jot the stories down in a journal—whatever it takes to pass them on to the generations that follow us.

CHAPTER 10

BLESSED CATASTROPHE

GINNY'S STORY

Steve called me from Quito. Just hearing his voice still excites me. He has proved to be the man of my dreams. But this time my enthusiasm came to an abrupt end when he casually mentioned to me that he was going to keep the apartment in Quito. Aunt Rachel had used the apartment when she was fighting cancer; it was the place her dear old body finally gave out and died.

But why would Steve be keeping the apartment? All my womanly intuition led to just one conclusion: *We are going back to live in Ecuador.* Alarms sounded, my chest constricted, I felt like I couldn't catch my breath. I'm sure the warm welcome in my voice died. Steve tried to assure me that it didn't mean anything.

"It for sure doesn't mean that we are moving back to Ecuador," he tried to convince me. I think he actually believed that. But I had not loved him and lived with him for more than twenty years without knowing something about how my man functions. I really don't think that he knew what was happening. He just felt that he should keep the apartment for a while, just in case.

I don't think Steve ever spent a single night in the apartment, but it would be a physical tie between us and Ecuador. I knew part of Steve's heart remained in Ecuador, where he was born and had grown up. But this new tie required paying rent and making decisions. Making new decisions about Ecuador scared me, and I couldn't hide it.

I knew something about Ecuador. I had met Steve there when he was the tour guide for a singing group tour I had been part of. Steve was only with us for three days, but even before those wonderful days were over—after just one talk with him, I knew.

God, I had prayed, *I never want to marry anyone unless he is like Steve Saint.* I guess it was easier for God to just let me marry the original, which is exactly what happened after a short six-month romance.

When I first moved to Ecuador, I lived with Steve's mom and stepdad. They treated me like family, but it was pretty intimidating living in a foreign country, working in a Spanish-speaking hospital, and living with people who would be my future in-laws. That was my introduction to Ecuador.

When my parents gave their blessing for me to marry Steve three months after my arrival in Ecuador, they told us they could not come down for a wedding for quite a while. My younger brother had already planned his own wedding, and it would be months before Mom and Dad could travel to Ecuador to see us. Steve convinced Dad that it would make perfect sense for us to get married before they came to visit. That way, by the time Mom and Dad came, we could all tour the country, including the jungles, together. I know Dad loved the idea of hunting with Steve and his Waodani friends. So Steve and I got married right away.

It was wonderful but inconvenient. I was working in Quito at Hospital Vos Andes, where Steve had been born. But Steve's construction projects were way out north of the city. We weren't seeing much of each other, and we could hardly stand it.

As quickly as possible, Steve had a door and windows installed in one room of the lower level of the house he was building for his parents. The house sat high on a ridge and overlooked a beautiful valley with a giant snowcapped mountain on the other side. I pictured living out there with Steve all alone, and I didn't care that we were going to be living in a house under construction.

I overlooked the little fact that all sixty of the workers lived there too. Steve wasn't just their employer, he was also their "patron," which meant that he furnished them with housing, food, and whatever else they needed. When their wives were going to have babies, Steve helped with the deliveries. When they got in trouble, Steve bailed them out of jail. This twenty-two-year-old husband of mine was their "godfather." I didn't mind that, but I wasn't sure I was ready to be their "godmother."

As soon as I moved out to the construction site, I found out I was pregnant. I was so sick that some days I just stayed in bed. That was just as well, because there were sixty men walking around, over, and through my one-room house at all hours of the day and night. We had no electricity, no kitchen, and worst of all, no bathroom. I actually dreamed of having a toilet to throw up in. Steve was obviously madly in love with me, but it was just as obvious that he had never been pregnant, living a quarter of a mile from the nearest working bathroom.

As planned, my parents came down to visit. It was wonderful getting to show them some of my new life. Steve and his enthusiastic employees had partially finished off a much larger room upstairs—with an even better view, a bathroom that worked, and a fireplace—in time for Mom and Dad's visit. If it had not been for an infestation of fleas that ate us alive in our new quarters, everything would have been blissful, in spite of the fact that we were still newlyweds sharing a room with my parents.

Our visit to the jungle went well. We spent most of the time with Steve's aunt Rachel at the Wycliffe base on beautiful Lake Limoncocha. It reminded me of hot, humid summer days in Minnesota. I liked that.

Steve and my dad got along great. With a little help from the Waodani, Steve and Dad brought howler monkeys home for our dinner. Dad was so proud, but Mom was startled when she lifted the lid off our cooking pot and discovered a monkey head grinning up at her.

While we were at Limoncocha, Mom, Dad, and I flew with Steve and Rachel to visit Rachel's home with the Waodani. I expected more Limoncocha. But this did not remind me of a Minnesota summer or anything else familiar. After we landed, Steve introduced my parents and me to the Waodani. They just stood and looked at us. Then they all gave what seemed to be a running commentary of what they thought of us, gesticulating and laughing uproariously. I felt like an animal in a zoo.

We were only there for a couple of hours, but it left an impression on me. Steve might belong to the Waodani, but I didn't. And I had no idea how to bridge not only the language barrier but the cultural one as well. It was a totally new experience for me. Maybe it was just too short a visit to break the ice, but I felt very uncomfortable.

I realize now that the total language barrier was primarily responsible for my discomfort. How do you make friends with people you can't talk to? The Waodani were probably waiting for me to show them some gesture of acceptance, while I was waiting for the same from them.

Unfortunately, that discomfort didn't go away during my next visit to the Waodani either. This visit took place in 1992, when most of Steve's extended family traveled into the jungles to attend the dedication of the Waodani New Testament. Rachel had worked on the translation for years, until Cathy Peek, Rosi Jung, and other Wycliffe translators finished the huge task.

It was a very special occasion, and we all wanted to be there. Steve and I brought our four children. Steve's sister, Kathy, also attended, along with one of her two sons. And Steve's brother, Phil, and his wife, Karla, brought their two boys.

Steve's friend Sam—or *Caento,* as the Waodani call him—offered to let us use his large house just twenty-five minutes by trail from Aunt Rachel's little house in Tonampade, the community next to "Palm Beach." Steve understood how important it had been to me to try to fit in with the Waodani on the last visit, and he decided it would be more comfortable for us to stay at Sam's place rather than right in the village.

Paa, one of Steve's childhood Waodani friends, had a house by Sam's. He looked out for us. Paa, whose parrot had been taken by one of the warriors and given to the missionaries in one of the bucket drops, was very friendly. I felt comfortable with him and his wife and their children.

We spent the last night before flying out of the jungles at

Rachel's house in the village. There, we were surrounded again by Waodani. I wanted so badly for them to know that I wanted to be their friend, but I felt totally inadequate. I couldn't tell them anything. And I couldn't understand a single word they were saying. It would have been different if I had just been a visitor who was going to meet them and leave. Then I would have cared much less that I couldn't communicate with them. And it probably would not have mattered nearly as much when they inspected me and seemed to be laughing about what they were seeing. They didn't hide the fact that they were laughing at us. I felt smothered.

Now, two and a half years later, the idea of moving back to Ecuador scared me to death. Steve might not be planning to move back, but I had the feeling it was a distinct possibility anyway.

When I first met Steve, I was immediately taken with him. I liked his blond hair and cowboy legs, but I was also drawn to the serious side of him. He seemed to know what was important in life and never felt that it would be any less exciting or rewarding to do what God wanted for him than what he wanted for himself. I was interested in him, but there was no way that I was going to make that interest known. I knew there could be nothing between us because in three days he would go back to his world and I would go back to mine. Our paths would probably never cross again.

On one of our outings, Steve took our group to visit a tea plantation that was quite deep in the jungles. Steve took off through the plantation, expecting us to follow. The boys in the group did a pretty good job at keeping up, but most of the girls were falling behind. It was then that I felt God telling me to show Steve that I would be willing to go anywhere with him. It was very strange. I have brothers and know something about how boys think. If I wanted to get Steve's attention, it would have made a lot more sense to fix my hair or pick out a cute outfit. But show a boy I hadn't even talked to that I could and would go anywhere with him? That didn't make any sense. The feeling was so strong, however, that I did it.

Soon it was just Steve, some of the boys from the group, and me. We had left all of the other girls and some of the boys behind.

Steve told me later that he was impressed that I was willing to slog through the mud at the tea plantation and did not give up when the other girls did. He also admitted that my ambition wasn't all he noticed. He also noticed when I climbed up the back of a surprise "Amazon camel" that had been left behind by a small visiting circus. And he noticed when I climbed over a chain-link fence in spite of the long dress I was wearing. He didn't realize that I had once been a little ragamuffin living on a small farm outside of our rural town.

After we were married, Steve told me that he had figured I was a Louis L'Amour kind of girl, the kind he could ride the river with. I knew that if we went back to Ecuador, however, it would not be a return to the mountains. I knew it would mean going to live with the Waodani out in the jungles.

Steve wasn't willing to say so, and maybe he didn't know yet, but I felt more and more sure that God's next assignment for him included a return to the jungle. I didn't want to hold him back. But I just could not go with him. I couldn't be a wife there. I couldn't be a mother there. I knew I would not even be able to function. I would just be a hindrance.

On the other hand, Steve couldn't function without me or someone like me. He can juggle a lot of balls at the same time and has a lot of good ideas. But if there isn't someone loyal with him to pick up the pieces and believe in him and take care of him, he will just go until he dies or gets locked up.

Steve assured me that if God did not clearly show both of us that we should go back to Ecuador, our answer would be to not go. But I was convinced that this wasn't Steve's whim. I believed it was God's leading—but only for Steve.

Polygamy fleetingly passed through my mind as a possible solution—not really. Then I realized that if I died, it would solve everything. Steve could marry someone more suited to the situation, someone who didn't mind feeling helpless and unable to communicate.

Don't get me wrong; it wasn't just that I didn't want to go to Ecuador. I already knew something about adverse circumstances. When Steve had asked me to leave my job and move to Ecuador the first time, I did it without question. I had moved with him to Quito, Willmar, Minneapolis, Wheaton, Grand Rapids, Quito (a second time), Dallas, Orlando, and Mali. In fact, when we were in West Africa, the country was in the middle of a terrible famine. People were dying from malnutrition, cholera, and other epidemics. We lived in a culture where we not only stood out, but where many people were antagonistic toward us. But even in Mali, I had a sink, a market from which to buy food, and a place to wash clothes.

Since I met Steve, I have never wanted to be anything as much I've wanted to be his wife and my children's mother. And I had been pretty good at it up till now. But I simply did not know how I could function without a stove, a refrigerator, running water, electricity, stores, telephones, mail, cars, knowledge of the language, familiar customs, or a bathroom. God had called me to be Steve's wife and my children's mother, and those were the tools I needed to do my job. I could get by without some of those things. But without any of them, I simply couldn't. I didn't just *feel* that I could not live in the middle of the Amazon; I *knew* it.

In my desperation, though, I remembered how God had told me to show Steve that I could go anywhere with him. My instructions didn't have anything to do with showing him that I could *do* anything, just that I could go anywhere. I realized that if I couldn't go live in the jungles, then I had misrepresented myself. And if that prompting had come from God, then God had been my accomplice. It really had not been my idea to try to impress Steve by trudging through the jungle. I definitely would have done it another way. If the idea was from God, I realized, then He would make a way for me to go and survive in the jungle.

I remembered something that Elisabeth Elliot had once said about going with Aunt Rachel to live with the Waodani. Because she couldn't speak the language and couldn't be of much help in terms of medical treatment, she wondered why God would call her back into the jungles. "If five men had been killed, who *could* succeed? But I could be obedient," she said.

I did believe Steve should go back to Ecuador, and I needed to be with him. God had made us a team. Although I still felt I could not function in the jungle as the wife and mother God had called me to be, I could not get Betty's words out of my mind. I couldn't do much, but I could obey.

When I turned that corner, I didn't have any better idea what would happen or what I would do. But something profound had happened. I felt peace. I didn't understand, but I felt it just the same, and I was confident it was a sign from God that He would see me through the ordeal ahead.

In January 1995, Steve and I made a quick visit to the Waodani. During that visit, reality hit me head-on. All the feelings of inadequacy came back, and I ended up crying and becoming undone in the middle of a Waodani party—just when I so badly wanted to show Steve that we could come as a team.

I knew that when we moved there, I would be watched and examined by the Waodani. They would expect me to help them, and I wouldn't be able to. After breaking down in despair, I really just wanted to go back to Rachel's house next to the tiny, tin-roofed Waodani church. Steve had already gone back, and I just wanted to be with him. But the young people, especially the girls, would not let me go. They had been singing choruses, and before I started to cry, I had taught them a few in English. They just kept begging me to do it again: *ayae, ayae, ayae adoki*—again, again, do it again.

They especially liked the songs with hand and body motions and lines like "Pharaoh, Pharaoh, Oh baby, let my people go." The Waodani were hilarious. Everyone did the motions in a different order, and no one knew what the words meant. But they loved doing it over and over again.

It wasn't much. It wouldn't take care of Steve or Stephenie, Jesse, Jaime, or Shaun. But at last I had found something I could offer. I could at least teach the Waodani to sing Christian choruses.

And so I prepared to leave our home, malls, appliances, friends, and extended family—everything familiar. And I was excited about it. I might as well have been on my way to the guillotine in the French Revolution. No, maybe that would have been easier. At least then I would have known that what

I was facing would soon be over. Here, I had little idea what I was about to face and no idea at all, really, how long it would last. But I could be obedient.

———

When we finally arrived in the jungle to live, Steve and the boys had only had a week to build us a house. Fortunately, some of Steve's Waodani friends pitched in. Construction down there starts with finding a tree, felling it, and then cutting it into boards with a chain saw. Steve was hesitant for me to see our new home until there was more to it. But I wanted to be with my men. Finally Steve agreed to move Stephenie and me from Shell to Nemompade, Star Creek, our new home.

I could tell Steve was nervous as we walked along the muddy trail from the little airstrip to where he and a couple of Waodani were building the first Nemompade houses. As we broke out of the dense jungle into the tiny clearing on the high bank that overlooked the Ewenguno (Curaray) River, Steve looked at me like a little boy delivering his report card. I wanted to be pleased for him. And when I looked at the crude framework built of chainsawed boards—no walls, no windows or doors, and just one little corner nine feet above the jungle floor with some rough boards for a floor under a tarp roof stretched over bamboo rafters—I *was* pleased. I can't explain it. I realized the issue had never been what I would or would not have. I had simply been afraid of being helpless. Once I got past that, I was content to live wherever in whatever.

Of course, there were still some aspects of jungle life that took a while to get used to. The meat came with skin on, still bleeding, and sometimes even quivering. The dress code was very casual. Men wore almost anything. Women usually wore a skirt and some kind of blouse. But occasionally one would show up with only a half-slip on. She would look at me and say, "My clothes are wet." Or she would use the expression *duranibai*—like the ancient ones.

When we went down to the stream behind the house or down to the river in front to bathe, some of our neighbors got real *duranibai*. The relaxed dress code was not immoral, and it wasn't sensual like it is in the States. In fact, I found it rather refreshing. Pretty soon, even our clean clothes were all mildewed and stained. We were integrating.

But there was one thing I just could not get used to. We never, ever had privacy. As we added more and more floorboards to the house, more and more Waodani came to visit. After a while, I got to know our neighbors and even started to get attached to those we lived with. Having *them* around all the time didn't seem like an invasion of privacy. But there were also Waodani who frequently visited from other communities. They all seemed to end up in our house too.

They came for medicine and medical attention. Tementa, Tidi, and some of the other men closed in an area under our house to serve as their pharmacy, and Mincaye's daughter Omanka and her son Mincaye (Jr.) ran it. The visiting Waodani also asked for nails, machetes, boots, flour, sugar, salt, soap, and other things that they had come to need and want. A few of them had money, but most of them wanted to trade artifacts for the things they needed.

I was glad we could help, but our house was becoming the "mall," and we were the only game in town. Coming to buy things was not a goal to be accomplished quickly. It was a happening—entertainment. One person at a time would ask for one thing at a time, a pound of small nails, for instance. Once that transaction was done, the person would remember that she needed a bar of soap. Then she needed some chloroquine for malaria, and we would have to call Omanka to open the pharmacy. Then she wanted boots but didn't have any more money. As soon as I put the boots away, she would produce a pig-tooth necklace to sell to us, which meant that she now had money for more goods.

Imagine trying to do that while you are also trying to fix supper on a camp stove and skin the hindquarter of a wild pig that is bleeding all over your rough two-board counter. That I never got used to.

Even when Tementa finally closed in more of the area under the house for a trading post, the visitors who came from other villages knew that we could show videos on the little twelve-inch, twelve-volt TV/VCR Steve and Jesse had rigged up. I frequently went to bed not knowing how many people would even be sleeping in our house that night.

Entertaining "outsiders" was a much bigger challenge. Unlike the Waodani, visitors from outside the jungle did not bring their own blankets. They rarely brought their own food, either. And they expected to sleep in beds instead of happily sprawling on our board floor. When we did occasionally have outside guests, the word would get out and people would often come from a number of other villages to get in on the fun.

One time, Steve brought a couple in to help wire up our solar panels to some golf cart batteries. This would allow us to call the United States by radio and power our computer and tiny printer when we needed to. The couple brought a friend who had obviously never been in the jungle before. She came in looking like she was going out for dinner in the city. Unfortunately, our pet wild pig met her at the airstrip and walked between her legs as she climbed out of the airplane. Her beautiful off-white slacks were dripping with mud from the puddle our pig had been lying in to keep cool while he waited for Steve to land.

When she got down to the river, the young woman attempted to wade into the river to wash off all the pig's mess. Instead, she slipped in the mud on the bank and fell flat on her back. She got most of that washed off in the river, but it meant that her only clothes were dripping wet as the sun went down. To the Waodani, this was wonderful entertainment. They probably discussed at length why the woman had lain in the mud on the bank and then tried to wash it off. If she wanted the mud on in the first place, why wash it off? It would not have occurred to them that she thought the bank was dry. Even the jungle children knew that the dry crust was only a fraction of an inch deep, covering a foot or more of thick goo.

Our outside guests found the Waodani amusing too. One of our guests wondered why every once in a while women would lay their nursing children face down on our floor. I had to explain that this was the only way mothers could be sure that the little boys' "nozzles" were aimed between the cracks in our floor. Both sides were entertained.

<hr>

The house was full. Everyone was happy. I would have enjoyed it too, if it had not been so wearying. Odae, our pet wild pig, was a nuisance, but he always kept things lively, treeing children and clacking his teeth at them. If the Waodani had not kept breaking his teeth off, he would have killed or maimed some of the children who constantly pestered him. He didn't threaten my life, but rather, my sanity. He chased our few chickens and would have eaten them if they hadn't been so fast. Chickens that can't fly don't live long in the jungles. Chickens that can fly are not much good to eat, unfortunately. Odae also had a bad habit of lying on my laundry, and he loved to eat whole bars of my soap. I came to hate that pig. But I didn't want to object because the Waodani had given him to us. I found out later that as soon as we left, the Waodani women made the men kill that wretched pig. They had tolerated him only because they thought I liked him.

We also had a monkey that lived on our front porch. He had a bad habit of attacking our legs without warning when we entered or left the house. We had to tie him up to keep him from living in the house. Two other monkeys were also given to us.

Stephenie had another pet, a night monkey who would prowl around our house beams waiting to pounce on our heads. It could leap long distances and had very soft, bulbous fingers and bushy hair. But when it pounced on my head from several feet up, it startled me, which in turn startled it. That usually resulted in my having to urgently wash my hair.

We also had a couple of macaws and some messy baby toucans. They loved to eat papaya or banana but usually began depositing it on our porch before they were done eating their fill.

One thing I thought I had going for me was that I had always had a pretty strong immune system—until we moved to the jungles, that is. Once we were living out there, we all got frequent systemic infections. Without warning, every little bite or scratch would become infected.

Then I started to get malaria on a somewhat regular basis. It was like the worst flu I had ever had, times three or four.

During my third bout with malaria, I stayed in bed for five days with fever and chills just waiting for the medicine to take effect.

Before I had gotten sick, Steve had scheduled a team to come in and do some filming for us. The day they arrived was my first day out of bed. I could not imagine having two or three additional men in our house. I barely had the energy to get up. But this had been planned for months, so I decided that I would just struggle through it. I soon realized that the struggle would be more than I'd bargained for: They were going to be with us for an entire week. When Steve told me that he planned to use the same flight taking them out of the jungles to bring our Easter guests in, it nearly pushed me over the edge.

I was so tired, I knew I'd never be able to put a smile on my face and soldier on. So when the team arrived, I received them as well as I could, thankful that Tidi had brought us a big hunk of catfish for their first dinner. Steve tried to encourage me. He realized I was weak and offered to help Stephenie prepare the food. But Steve was the center of all sorts of things going on in the village. The thought of him leaving those things to do what I was supposed to do—and wanted to do—was unthinkable.

I quickly excused myself and went to bed, too exhausted and weak to even think about the next day's challenges. I couldn't help but think about the Bible verse that says each day has enough trouble of its own. As I lay there in bed, I kept going back to that verse and thinking, *How true it is*. I was absolutely done in, without having done much of anything. As I went to sleep, I asked God to give me the strength I needed and to help me be sweet.

The next morning, I woke up early and forced myself out of bed. I had to make something for breakfast for all of us.

The Waodani eat the same thing for breakfast that they eat for lunch and dinner, but *cowodi* aren't really used to eating manioc and catfish for breakfast. So we usually made oatmeal or pancakes for outside guests. Steph and I decided to make pancakes, which aren't too complicated to prepare, even in the jungle. But after that small chore, I was exhausted again.

I waited for the film team to leave the house so I could lie back down. The malaria fever was gone, but the lethargic, empty, no-energy feeling was just as acute as ever. When ten o'clock rolled around and our guests were still just sitting in the living center of our small house enjoying themselves—not even getting ready to leave—I was beside myself. I could hardly stand up. I wanted to scream at them, but I was desperately trying to still act sweet. I wanted so badly to be a positive reflection on Steve, who always tells me that meeting a man's wife tells more about him than any résumé could.

It was a Sunday, and Steve had gone to the informal church service in the village, so I was left to entertain the group myself. On top of everything else, one of the men seemed to be oblivious to the fact that everyone else had left their boots on the porch. Jungle boots have a heavy tread that is almost perpetually filled with mud from the trail. In the house, the mud dries and then the boots shed clumps of mud all over. Even those Waodani who lived on dirt floors knew enough to wipe the mud off their feet before entering a house, whether its floors were dirt or boards. *Oh God, help me be sweet, and forgive me for my bad attitude,* I prayed over and over.

Finally Steve returned, and the group set out to film the felling of a huge tree in Odae's clearing (Odae is a warrior, whose name means *wild pig*). At last I could lie down again. I knew I could not keep this up. I began to pray even more fervently now. I was truly desperate. Not only was I sick, but I was also dreadfully lonely. Steve couldn't spend time with me, and I was terribly scared that I would embarrass him and myself by being an ungracious hostess. I simply did not know what to do but pray.

After I had been in bed only a short time, I felt the house shake. Someone was coming. I could tell that it was Steve, but I knew that the film crew couldn't have gotten to the garden, filmed the tree being cut, and returned already. I also knew that they had planned to do more filming while they were upriver, too.

Oh God, no, I prayed. *They can't be coming back so soon.* I couldn't tell Steve how desperate I was. What if he felt he had to take the men away for my sake? I would never live down the shame.

I opened my eyes to find Steve standing above me, just looking at me. I knew from the look in his eyes that he could tell I was desperate. But what he said did not fit that look.

"Ginny, have you been praying?" he asked.

"Why do you ask? Did something happen? Did you almost get killed?" I blurted out, not even sure where that thought had come from.

"No, I didn't, but the cameraman almost did. Tidi was felling the tree with his big chain saw. I told the cameraman where to stand, but he wanted to shoot from a much closer spot, at least until the tree was close to falling," Steve began. "When the cameraman was set, Tidi started to cut some more. Suddenly the saw plunged all the way into the tree, and I heard a terrible noise. The inside of that tree was hollow, and with one huge crack, it broke where Tidi had been cutting and began a breathtakingly fast plunge to earth.

"I took one glance and saw that it was going to fall right where the camera recorder was sitting. The cameraman was ready to lunge for it. I screamed, 'Nooooo!' and that huge tree landed directly on top of the recorder. It drove the entire thing into the ground and would have done the same to the cameraman if he had grabbed for it. Everyone is alive, but that video recorder is no more."

Without their recorder, there was nothing left for the team to do, and Steve flew the men into Shell the very next morning. This will sound heartless, but God could not have shown His personal understanding and care to me in a more sensitive way than He did that day in Nemompade. I was still weak, but there was a song in my heart. It wasn't because the men were gone or because I felt well again. It was because I felt loved.

That Tuesday was my forty-fifth birthday. It was sunny, and the humidity was down to about 95 percent. Steve stayed in Shell to do some maintenance on our little airplane, so there were few visitors other than our Nemompade neighbors who were all close friends of mine by now. I rested and got some of my strength back. I washed out two big baskets of clothes, sheets, and towels down at the creek and dried them the same day. It was wonderful. I didn't even want to kill our wild pig that day. Well, maybe I exaggerate a bit there.

I was lighthearted and almost twirled one of my startled neighbors. It was as though God had said, *Ginny Lynn, I love you so much. I see what you are going through and I care. I knew you needed a break; enjoy it!*

For the first time in my life I thought, *I need to build a monument to remember this wonderful experience. I cannot forget this kindness God just did for me.*

When Steve came in with our new guests, we had a wonderful Easter with them and with our Waodani family. And when I told Steve about what had happened, he agreed that God had done this just for me. A couple of years later, he began talking about the importance of recording our sand castles for our children and grandchildren, and I knew this was one of mine.

I thought I couldn't survive in the jungle where I would be totally helpless. I thought I needed to help the Waodani. Instead, I learned that I could do more for them by allowing them to help me. I also thought that I needed to help God. Instead, I learned in a much deeper way just how much He loves and cares for me. God took that moment of great weakness and turned it into one of the highlights of my spiritual journey.

I still feel a bit sheepish that God's kindness to me meant the end of a very expensive video recorder. But that was God's doing, and I felt the warmth of it to my very core. Even all these years later, I still can't think about what God did without tearing up. I know He, who created the stars with just the power of His word, loves little old Ginny Lynn. That warms my heart.

CHAPTER 11

END OF THE SPEAR

Have you ever thought about what it would be like to be a movie star? It is embarrassing to admit it now, but I remember looking in the mirror after discovering "butch wax," which would make my short blond hair stand up in front, and thinking that I looked like Timmy in the *Lassie* television series.

Well, stardom never happened for me. At least not like I imagined it might when I was very young. I did, however, get to participate in making a movie. Until *End of the Spear*, I had no idea what a huge undertaking it is to make a major motion picture.

End of the Spear is set in Ecuador, on the western bulge of South America that sits directly south of New York City. To make the movie realistic, we needed to film in real jungles. I lobbied for it to be shot right in Ecuador, but that was before I knew what was involved. By the time filming began in the jungles in Panama, I realized why it would have been impossible to shoot in Ecuador. There were just short of three hundred people involved: actors, makeup artists, costume people, camera operators, sound technicians, electricians, food service providers, a stunt director, and logistics managers, along with a host of car, van, and truck drivers—and all their assistants and helpers. There were also the writers, directors, producers, set builders, and special effects people.

The film crew worked an average of twelve hours per day, six days a week. When they were off work, they still had to eat, do laundry, keep track of families and businesses back in the United States, sleep, and then get ready for the next day's challenges. At the end of a long day of hard, hot work, an air-conditioned hotel did not seem like a luxury. It was a necessity. In the Ecuadorean jungle, the crew would have had to sleep on cots or hammocks in temporary shelters. I quickly realized that people would have simply worn out and the movie never would have been finished. Shooting in Panama created its own challenges, however. There was a beautiful hotel made from a converted U.S. military hospital. There were roads for the fleet of cars and trucks required to move people and equipment around the various sets. There were cell phone and radio capabilities to keep everyone in touch with each other. But there were no Waodani.

It would have been daunting, if not impossible, to bring enough Waodani men, women, and children from Ecuador to Panama to fill all the movie parts for three months. So the casting director found a tribal group in Panama that he thought resembled the Waodani. The Panamanian Embera would play the parts of Ecuadorean Waodani. When I heard that the Embera were very similar to the Waodani both in appearance and custom, I was skeptical.

To people of one race, members of another tend to look alike. Mincaye, one of the warriors who killed Dad and his friends, and I did speaking tours together. One day, during one of those events, we spoke in three consecutive services in the same church. When we went onstage for the second service, Mincaye asked, "Are these foreigners not listening to us?"

"They are listening very well to our talk," I answered. The people had been so attentive that I had gone over our allotted time. Mincaye seemed to be satisfied by my answer that the audience *was* listening.

But in the third service Mincaye looked out at the audience and stated, "These foreigners are *not* listening to us well." I finally realized what he was thinking.

"Mincaye, these are different *cowodi.*"

He looked out at the audience again very carefully and said, "Really? They all look the same." Tribal people tend to look the same to *cowodi* too.

When I expressed my concern that the Embera might not resemble Waodani people, the film crew asked me to accompany a group of them to visit the Embera. From Panama City, we took a bus to the Chagres River just above where it empties into the Panama Canal. There we were met by several Embera men in a large dugout canoe. I was surprised to see that the canoe was very similar to the canoes that the Waodani make. When we neared the Embera village of Parara Puru, the engine on the back of the canoe was cut off, and several of the men grabbed poles to propel us the last hundred feet or so to the dirt bank below the village.

The first thing that struck me when we arrived was that the men wore G-strings just like the Waodani used to. The distinction was that the Embera men used their waist strings to support a bright loincloth that hung down in front. Waodani men's traditional dress consisted solely of the multistranded waist string. The Embera women wore brightly colored skirts that the Waodani women would have loved. But the only cloth the Waodani had in the old days was rough bark cloth that they used as slings to carry their babies in. From the waist up, however, the Embera women's and Waodani women's costumes were identical.

As the Embera line danced for us, I began to realize that some of the Embera actually looked like Waodani people I knew. In fact, I took some pictures of several of the Embera, which I showed to the Waodani on my next trip to Ecuador. Even the Waodani thought that a couple of the Embera were actually Waodani.

To be as authentic as possible, the film crew asked me to take a delegation of Waodani to Panama to show the Embera cast how to truly act like the Waodani "ancient ones." The Emberas' ancestors were also hunter-gatherer-gardeners, but the Embera who would be acting in *End of the Spear* were several generations removed from that lifestyle. The Embera near Panama City lived primarily off of the tourist trade. They had maintained those aspects of their culture that visitors would find attractive and that could easily be demonstrated to tourists in their village.

The Waodani would need to teach them to throw spears, shoot blowguns, sleep in string hammocks, and climb trees with climbing vines. The young Embera who were chosen to act in the movie realized that these were skills their ancestors had mastered. They were excited to learn, and the Waodani teachers were capable and enthusiastic.

By the time filming actually began in early January 2004,

the Embera actors and the Waodani teachers had built quite a rapport. By contrast, the North American members of the film crew were professional and courteous to the Waodani, but we rarely came in contact with them. I did get the idea, however, that the professionals were at least mildly cynical about the actual truth of the story they were filming.

I suppose that to most people, it would seem unnatural and maybe even inappropriate for me to closely associate with those who brutally killed my dad, much less love and accept them as family. And I'm sure that most of the crew was used to working on scripts that were adapted from novels or other real-life stories. Most such adaptations take a great deal of creative license so that in the end, the movie only vaguely resembles the true story. This was not the case with *End of the Spear*, but they didn't know that yet.

When the three-month shoot was nearly finished, something happened on the set that proved the film's veracity. It occurred while we were filming the reenactment of Aunt Rachel's funeral. As we prepared for the scene, I wanted to be sure that it was visually and materially as accurate as possible.

After living with the Waodani for thirty-six years, Aunt Rachel had died on November 11, 1994. When I got the call, I immediately jumped on a plane and headed to Ecuador to help my jungle family bury my dear old aunt, who had been like a second mother to me.

The Gikitaidi, the Waodani clan that had killed my dad and his four friends, were the same Waodani who had accepted Aunt Rachel and Elisabeth Elliot. Many of them deeply loved Aunt Rachel and had become family to her. I wanted to make sure that they were in charge of this final act of burying *Nemo*—Star—as they called her. I wanted to ensure that this was *their* farewell. I asked that only those outsiders who had good reason to be at the funeral deep in Waodani territory attend. In a final effort to show respect for Rachel's closest "relatives" in the tribe, I took the nails that were going to be used to nail the lid on her coffin and gave one to each of her closest tribal friends.

They each drove a nail into the crude coffin, and several of them spontaneously eulogized this ruddy-complected foreigner they had loved. I still feel a tug at my heart when I think of Kimo's words: "Teaching us to walk God's trail, Star came." The movie script called for this scene to be reenacted just as it had happened. The set crew built a very close replica of Aunt Rachel's little jungle hut and the rustic church building next door. But Jim Hanon, the director, wanted to make this scene even more special. He decided to include some of the actual people from the story. Although their parts were played by actors in the movie, he would use them as extras in this scene.

So I was asked to arrange for another delegation of Waodani to travel from Ecuador to Panama. This second delegation had widely varying degrees of exposure to the outside world. Mincaye, who had traveled extensively with me, was practically a world traveler. But others had probably never even been out of the jungle. Everything was new for them: getting on buses and in and out of cars; eating in restaurants; taking showers; and using electric lights, washing machines, elevators, and telephones. This was an entirely new world.

There were a few things that were familiar to them: the replica of *56 Henry* and the howler monkeys that created chaos every time they began their thunderous calling in the trees near our apartment. The Waodani desperately wanted to get their hands on the blowguns they had made for the movie so they could kill and eat those fat Panamanian primates. We probably would have all ended up in jail if they had, but I knew it would do no good to warn them of that possibility. When I had tried to explain the concept of incarceration to Mincaye, he actually got excited. What could be more wonderful than being locked in a little house with a television and three meals a day where you never had to work in the garden or walk steep, muddy trails?

I'm not sure this group of Waodani actually understood what was happening on the movie sets. The complexities of shooting a movie were perplexing even to those of us who had been watching movies all our lives. Everything that was going on had to be coordinated in minute detail. Actors who had to have false earlobes and earplugs applied each day could take a long time in makeup. Costumes had to be ready for each scene. Then there were the lights and cameras. Many of the shots required that the camera be able to move with an actor. That may not be very difficult in a studio shoot, but on the rough jungle floor it required clearing vegetation and leveling the ground. The special effects people had to be able to make it rain on-set when the weather was bright and clear. And they had to make it bright and clear sometimes when it was actually raining on the set. This required covering the jungle canopy with giant rain tarps or using a huge artificial sun.

At between twelve and thirteen thousand dollars per hour, mistakes as simple as having too few spears on-set for a given scene could cost thousands of dollars. In one of the opening scenes in the movie, a string came loose from a bat's foot. That mistake cost about five thousand dollars while we rushed around in an old U.S. underground ammunition bunker trying to catch a replacement to finish the scene.

The burial scene was going to be one of the most complicated scenes in the movie, mostly due to the large number of actors and extras participating. The film crew had spent several hours getting this particular scene set up before calling the actors and extras into position. Instructions and practice runs took a significant amount of additional time. Finally, after what must have been a hundred thousand dollars' worth of preparation, they were ready to shoot this special scene.

Ginny and our son Jesse and his wife and one of our grandchildren were in the little rustic replica church, along with my sister and mother, two other widows, and two of Ed McCully's sons. Dayumae, Kimo, Mincaye, and Dyuwi were also there. But I could not be in the scene because my face had already been seen when I played the short part of Frank Drown, the man who led the search party to find out what had happened to my dad and his four friends.

Determined to be near the reenactment of this dramatic event that was still so fresh in my memory, I crawled under the little church that sat on squat cement posts. My head was only a foot beneath the coffin when I heard the director call, "Quiet on the set. Lights. Cameras."—each camera operator called that his or her equipment was rolling and up to speed—and then, "ACTION!"

They were just a short ways into the shoot when I could tell that the nails for Aunt Rachel's coffin lid were being distributed. I was reliving every detail. Then, totally without warning and completely unexpectedly, Dyuwi—the real Dyuwi—started talking in a loud voice that boomed over the other dialogue that was part of the script. I couldn't imagine what was going on.

I crawled out from under the building as fast as I could and climbed up the short outside wall to see what was happening.

Dyuwi, who was positioned right at the front of the church, had his hands raised in the air and was in the middle of a long and dramatic monologue. I realized from his tone of voice and his bowed head that he was praying. Dyuwi is a very shy man—except when he is praying. Then he forgets about everything that is going on around him and speaks to God as though volume will help carry his words to their divine destination.

Some of the extras probably thought this was part of the scene, but the film crew knew that it wasn't. I expected them to stop the cameras and cut the scene to start again. But they didn't. I think everyone was too surprised to react. No one knew what to do. They couldn't tell Dyuwi what to do—at least not in words that he would understand.

Then I noticed that Christina, the actress who was playing the role of Dayumae, had started to cry. I knew Dyuwi had just interrupted an important scene, but I couldn't figure out why Christina would be crying. The cost of reshooting the scene wasn't going to come out of her paycheck.

Christina's crying soon turned to sobbing. I had just realized that she wasn't offended by what Dyuwi was doing but was moved by it, when the real Dayumae stood up right behind Christina and put her arms around her in a tight embrace.

"That is just how I cried when we really buried *Nemo*," Dayumae tried to tell her. "But you don't have to cry. *Nemo* is not really dead; she has gone to live in *Waengongi's* (God's) place."

Christina accepted Dayumae's comfort and hugged her back as both of them now cried.

Just then, I heard the sound of additional crying coming from inside the coffin where Sara, who was playing Aunt Rachel, had just been sealed in with nails. Someone urgently called for a crowbar to open the coffin and set Sara free. But when they pried off the cover, Sara made no move to get out. By this time, it became apparent to everyone that Dyuwi had been overcome with emotion as he relived the actual events surrounding Aunt Rachel's funeral and what her life and message had meant to him. He just had to thank *Waengongi* for the life-changing message that had set him free from a life of hatred, vengeance, and fear. As he innocently thanked the Creator, he made a deep and profound impact on those of us who watched his act of thanksgiving.

Some of the people on-set that day were determined God followers. Many were not. I have no way of knowing if anyone on the set decided to turn from walking his or her own trail to walk God's trail because of what Dyuwi did. But I sensed a markedly different attitude toward the story after that on the part of the dedicated film crew.

I think it had finally sunk in. Certainly no one had prompted Dyuwi to interrupt a very complex and expensive scene. What he had done was purely a spontaneous reaction to the transformation that *Waengongi* had worked in his life, and he was expressing his gratitude for that change.

From then on, there seemed to be a subtle change in all of our attitudes toward the story we were working together to make into a movie. This wasn't just an embellished story that was exaggerating the mystical possibilities of transformation and reconciliation that God can work in people's lives. It was the real deal. The Waodani's love for the wives and families of the men they had once hated and killed was proof. The love of these families for the very Waodani who had killed their husbands and fathers and grandfathers doubled the evidence.

End of the Spear isn't just based on a true story. The story it tells really is true. And *Waengongi* is still in the transformation and reconciliation business. Hatred and a desire for revenge are natural emotions. Forgiveness and love for enemies are not. Acts of forgiveness and reconciliation are powerful signs of God along the way. We simply need to be ready and willing to be a part of them.

+

+

CHAPTER 12

I WONDERED IF I WOULD EVER SEE THAT LITTLE PLANE AGAIN

When we were shooting the interviews of the five widows for *Beyond the Gates of Splendor*, a documentary that parallels *End of the Spear*, something my mom said really stuck in my mind.

We had asked each of the widows to talk about the last time they had seen their husbands alive. Mom said, "We had been in this thing together from the very beginning. There was really nothing special left to say. But one thought crossed my mind as Nate taxied out from the hangar in front of our house." Here Mom began to cry as she remembered what happened that day and the significance it would have in her life. "I wondered if I would ever see that little airplane taxi out again." Mom took a short, dramatic pause and then she looked at the camera, tears still in her eyes. She shook her head in the negative. "I never did."

When I was a little boy, there was one particular possession that I most identified with. It helped me in a powerful way to understand who I was, yet it wasn't even completely mine. I shared it with my hero. It was N5156H, the Piper PA-14 little four-seat bush plane. To me it was the prettiest, fastest, most important airplane ever. After all, it was flown by the smartest, safest, strongest, bestest jungle pilot in the world.

When my dad flew away in *56 Henry* one day never to return, it was the most crushing, unthinkable, dark, and menacing thing that had ever happened in my little life.

I was not shown pictures of my dad's body at the memorial service that was held in our little town, Shell Mera, on the edge of the great Amazon jungle. All I saw was the lifeless body of *56 Henry*. Its vibrant yellow skin had been torn from its skeleton. One of its wings was hanging on the beach, unable to hold even its own fragile weight in "death." The engine—with the beautifully cool, smooth propeller with red tips that I loved to stroke when no one was watching—was gone too. No one had to tell me the details of what had been done to my hero. As I looked at what had been done to our mutual friend and confidant, faithful old *56 Henry*, I could tell what must have happened to Dad.

56 Henry, like my dad, was gone forever. And I felt the loss every time I stepped out of our house and saw the empty place in Dad's hangar. My life would never be the same without Dad and *56 Henry*.

56 Henry couldn't be given back to me. It was torn apart and its body parts had to be abandoned in "hostile territory." Over the years, aviation enthusiasts periodically tried to talk me into mounting a salvage operation to find the remains and make a missions memorial from them. For years I gave no more thought to that idea than I did to the idea of trying to locate my dad's remains. They were both part of a closed chapter, "brief candles," as Shakespeare wrote, that had spent their hour upon the stage and then were seen no more.

Then in 1994, Cawitipae, a Waodani warrior, and his wife did find *56 Henry*'s remains. They even found the little aluminum nameplate from Dad's plane that identified *56 Henry* as a Piper. Finding that little nameplate was one of the signs God used to convince me that *that* chapter wasn't really over. But that is another story.

The actual remains of good old *56 Henry* are now part of a missions memorial that are on display at the Mission Aviation Fellowship headquarters in Idaho. The *56 Henry* display is there to remind MAF visitors that the need that Dad and *56 Henry* were dedicated to half a century ago still exists today.

And yes, God did use my finding the remains of good old *56 Henry* to start the process of convincing Ginny and me that we should accept the Waodani's invitation to live with them after my aunt Rachel died. She had been the first outsider to have ever lived with the Waodani. When she died, she had been living with them for more than thirty-six years.

But I need to explain what that has to do with *56 Henry*. After our family spent a year and a half helping the Waodani try to take charge of meeting their own people's needs, we returned to the United States to fulfill a bigger vision they had. They wanted other frontier peoples like themselves to have access to the same training and equipping that they had so badly craved.

It was after we returned to the States that Mart Green contacted me about making a movie. Making a movie may sound exciting, but movies don't just happen; good scripts are fickle works of art, actors don't work for nothing, and people don't go to see movies or buy a DVD without lots of publicity. It is a long, complicated process that can be shot dead at any one of a hundred points along the way.

About halfway through that seven-year process of making the movie, one of the production team members said to me that they wanted to use an exact replica of my dad's plane in the movie. That caught my interest instantly.

Piper PA-14s are rare planes. "Where did you find one?" I asked.

"Oh, we don't have one yet. We don't need it for almost a year. But when we do, would you help us find one?"

They obviously had no idea how rare PA-14s are and how proud the owners are of the ones in flying condition that still exist. I explained to the executive producer that if they really expected to have a cub yellow PA-14 in original configuration within a year, we'd better start looking immediately. He asked me if I would look for one. I was excited to get involved in this very personal part of the movie project.

I began by getting a record of every PA-14 in the world that was still registered with the Federal Aviation Administration and then started calling their owners. Most owners just hung up as soon as I said, "I understand you have a PA-14." Apparently mine was not the first prospecting call they had received. The ones who didn't hang up just said, "It isn't for sale." One owner told me there wasn't enough money in the bank to buy his plane. Another one asked if I owned the bank.

"No," I told him. "But I own some stock, if that would help."

"That won't be enough," he said, and laughed as he hung up. Finally, I found a PA-14, the longtime owner of which had died. His widow sold the plane to a friend in Minnesota who took off the floats and put it back on wheels. I called the new owner and, to my surprise, N4225H was for sale.

The plane didn't have any legally working radios, and the cam needed to be replaced, which meant a major overhaul. The plane had been built in the 1940s, and most of the instruments looked like they could have been originals. The wingtips had been squared off for better performance, which meant they would have to be rounded off again to look like Dad's plane, and this plane was white with a red interior and red trim on the outside. Dad's plane had been painted a bright "Cub yellow" so it would be easier to find if he ever crashed in the jungles.

A friend of mine, who is a very experienced missionary pilot, agreed to test-fly the new-old plane with me. He had not flown a tail dragger for a long time, so we decided that I would fly as pilot and he would be copilot. I guess we were thinking that if something went wrong, two of us could come up with twice as many possible remedies, and if those remedies didn't work, we at least wouldn't be alone.

It was so cold in Minnesota in January that we had to put a heater under the engine and throw a big quilt over the engine to keep the heat in the engine compartment. We also needed to keep ourselves from freezing in the drafty cabin during our test flight.

We got the engine started okay, but we couldn't keep it running. Airplanes usually have two or more fuel tanks, and the pilot selects one of the tanks. It looked to me like the fuel selector was pointing to the right-wing tank. But I finally realized that on very old Pipers such as this one, the long pointer on the fuel selector is really the "tail." Opposite the long tail, a tiny raised arrow designates the actual position selected. Our problem with keeping the engine running was that the tail on our fuel selector was pointing to the right tank, but the arrow was pointing to *off*.

It is a good thing we didn't have any passengers. If they heard us exclaim, "Oh yeah, this knob points over here when we need to get gas, *I think*," I doubt they would have wanted to fly with us.

After deciding that the plane was good to go, I headed from Minnesota to Florida with my brother's son, Karl. We were dressed like we were going ice fishing. For navigation, we used a U.S. road atlas. It wasn't a GPS, but since we were flying low and slow with no radio to talk to anyone, it worked just fine. That was the way I had learned to fly.

Ice began to accumulate on the plane as we flew through freezing drizzle while crossing the border into Arkansas. Ice can wreak havoc with the flying characteristics of an airplane. That wasn't our only problem. The setting sun was also shining right in our eyes. It seemed like an opportune time to find a place to spend the night. While landing, I discovered that the brakes did not work right, nor did the tail wheel work right. With no steering, I could not keep the airplane on the runway. As we headed off the narrow country airstrip into the ditch that ran along the side, Karl calmly informed me, "Uncle Steve, I think we are going to hit the next runway light." We didn't, but it was close.

The next day the clouds were very low and we ended up flying down the Mississippi River to avoid running into towers and overpasses. We gave a couple of tugboat captains a scare when we flew by them. We were so low that I was actually looking *up* at one of those tug captains.

New Year's Eve found Karl and me at the north Florida border sleeping in a little terminal building at a county airport.

Our celebration consisted of some popcorn other pilots had left behind and some old movies the airport kept around for pilots like ourselves who were grounded by bad weather. But even with all these obstacles, it was exciting to be flying a plane like Dad's old PA-14. I imagined it painted yellow, flying over the emerald green jungle.

Months later, we finally had the new engine, propeller, brake system, instrument panel, and interior in PA-14 N4225H. It did not look much like *56 Henry*, however. The wings were still square, and it was still painted white with crimson trim. And it was still *25 Hotel* instead of *56 Henry*. Fortunately, some friends at a missionary aviation training program in Ohio were going to help us change that. When they were done, N4225H really had become *56 Henry*.

Once we finished rebuilding the new *56 Henry*, we had to dismantle it to ship it down to Panama in a container. I hated to have to take the plane apart, but we could not take the chance of having an engine failure while flying across the Caribbean. *56 Henry* was going to be a significant actor in the movie. No *56 Henry*, no movie—there were no more yellow PA-14s available to act as a stunt double.

In Panama, my friend Barry and I put *56 Henry* back together and got the plane ready for its movie debut. The film team found out that it wasn't going to be easy to find a stunt pilot who knew how to fly such an old plane. Flying the plane wasn't the biggest challenge. The *big* challenge was flying *56 Henry* in close formation with a helicopter camera ship in constant windy conditions in a Spanish-speaking country, over the waters of the Panama Canal—a high-security area. These factors combined made the job uninviting for other pilots. So they offered me the job.

I realized that I should probably pretend to think this over for a while. But I'm not that good of an actor. Would I fly *56 Henry* in the movie? You bet I would! *Wow!*

We built our own runways right next to the replica of my old house where I had watched Dad and *56 Henry* fly off for the last time so many years before. It was both emotional and exciting to taxi in between the rustic hangar and the beautiful old wooden house with its distinctive tin half roof between the first and second stories. Dad designed the half roof to keep driving jungle rains from blowing in our lower windows.

The very first flight with *56 Henry* in Panama was almost a showstopper. Martina, the aerial unit camera operator, wanted to get an idea of what it would be like to shoot from inside *56 Henry*. We took off the right door, and the grips rigged a mount so the large high-definition camera could shoot through the opening. This left just enough room for Martina to kneel on the small rear seat behind the camera.

First, Martina told me she wanted to see if she could shoot from inside the plane up into a tree line. There were a couple of scenes that called for Dad to see a Waodani warrior high in a jungle tree. I did not realize what Martina was after exactly, but in order to get that shot, I knew we would have to fly lower than the treetops. The obvious way to do that safely seemed to be to fly low over water shooting up into the trees along the shoreline.

Martina, "Big Bertha" (the camera), and I all crammed into *56*'s tiny cockpit, and I flew the short distance from the movie set out over the Caribbean before dropping down low over the water. The trees came right down to the waterline along the shore. That would help. But they were not very tall, so we had to fly very, very low—I'm talking about low enough that a large wave could have hit us.

Trimming the plane so that if I lost concentration and loosened my grip on the control stick the plane would climb rather than descend into the ocean, we skimmed over the waves along the vibrant green of the virgin jungle shoreline. There was a problem, however. I was so low that when the shoreline curved, I could not bank to turn as a plane is designed to do. I could only skid through the turns using extra rudder. It felt as if we were in a car trying to navigate a winding road covered in slick ice. But Martina seemed to love it. She had shot movie footage from a number of different aircraft, and this rig of ours didn't seem to bother her at all.

We were just settling into shooting our practice footage when, without any warning, the engine quit—dead. It did not lose power or sputter or cough. It just went immediately from a normal roar to dead silent. My mind raced, half of it trying to figure out what had happened and how to correct the problem, the other half imagining the impending loss of this irreplaceable plane.

As soon as the engine died, I instinctively relaxed the forward pressure on the joystick. With the nose trimmed up, the plane began to climb, but our speed bled off quickly, and I could tell that we were going to stall in just a few seconds. We were about to go swimming, and *56 Henry* didn't know how.

Just seconds before we began our plunge into the salty water that was only twenty feet below us now, *56 Henry* roared back to life. That was a beautiful sound. Along with the renewed roar of the engine, I could hear the wild beating of my heart. With all of that noise, I almost missed Martina's exclamations coming through my headphones.

"What was that? What happened? Are we okay? What are you going to do?" She had obviously taken note that something out of the ordinary had just happened. In practice sessions, Martina had given every indication that she really was fearless.

Now it seemed I had found her one weakness. As long as she was looking through the camera viewfinder, Martina was fearless. But just like Samson without his long hair, Martina became human without her camera. She wanted some answers. But I didn't have them to give to her.

I only knew that as soon as the engine quit, without even being conscious of what I was doing, I had instinctively switched the fuel selector from the right-wing tank to the left. The engine quit only one more time during our filming of *End of the Spear*. And it happened about ten minutes later. But I'm sure Martina would like to forget that incident, so I won't share it here. Let me just say that I now make a mental note that reminds me not to demonstrate "bucket drops" too soon after an engine failure unless the tank is at least half full.

Other flights weren't quite as dramatic, but they were certainly just as memorable for me. I got to fly *56 Henry* down river gorges, run the wheels on sandy beaches, and buzz a bird-watching tower sticking up through the jungle canopy. We also flew in the rain and just after it, to shoot the mysterious mists rising out of the jungle.

Whenever I landed back at Shell Mera, I gave *56* full left rudder, a touch of right brake, and a quick burst of power to make the tail swing around, ready to push back into the hangar—just like I used to see my dad do. After we had *56* settled down one night, I rubbed my hand across its smooth propeller with its freshly painted red tips, and it was almost like being a little boy again. The only thing I needed was to hear that almost forgotten voice say, "So how's *56 Henry* tonight, sonny boy?" and the scene would have been perfect.

The very pinnacle of the mountain for me, flying *56 Henry* Jr. in the movie, was the landing on Palm Beach. Boys often grow up with a "my dad" mentality: My dad is the strongest man in the world. My dad is the fastest runner in the world. My dad can do anything your dad can do—better—and on and on. But my dad was dead. I couldn't participate in the my-dad-is-bigger, better, burps more, throws me higher, etc. contest. But in my heart, I always harbored the assurance that my dad was the best jungle pilot ever. I had a short piece of film footage showing his precarious landing on tiny little Palm Beach to prove it. Growing up, I had watched Dad's incredible sliding approach down the narrow, winding Ewenguno River over and over again. Now I got to recreate that landing.

Unfortunately for me, the movie set people who picked Palm Beach in Panama did not know anything about landing planes on river sandbars. They were totally focused on duplicating the size of the river, the jungle look around it, and the serpentine course the real river took as it approached the beach. They were only looking for a beach that had enough room to stage *56 Henry* and the handful of actors that the scenes on the beach required. When they told me they had found the perfect beach, I asked how long it was.

They sent me pictures that showed where the scenes would be reenacted. Again, I asked how long the beach was. They wrote me a more complete description of how much like the Ewenguno the chosen river in Panama was. I asked more insistently how long the beach was. Someone wrote back in an attempt to quell any concerns I might have: "It's pretty long."

I wrote back, "Could you describe that in numbers of feet, please?" An assistant director finally responded that the beach was about four or five hundred feet long. *How much of it is usable?* I wondered. *Is it straight? Are the approaches good?* When I asked, no one knew. The fact that I was supposed to land a real plane on that little stretch of pebbles seemed to have slipped everyone's mind.

I got my answers a few days after arriving in Panama, when one of the movie team members took my friend Barry and me to see the beach for ourselves. We discovered that the "beach" was really two tiny beaches. Part of the river cut the first three hundred feet from the final hundred feet or so. Even if we could divert that part of the river, we would still have just over four hundred feet. Dad's little beach had been six hundred feet long.

In addition to being incredibly short, our beach had a dog-leg right in the middle. For people who only drive, the bend would not seem very important. But in landing a little airplane on a tiny sandbar, it was a very big deal.

It was not difficult to evaluate the landing approach to our "Palm Beach." On the downriver end, there was a stand of tall trees. On the upriver side, the site selection team was right: Our river looked just like the river Dad had twisted down to land on his beach—except that our river and beach were only about two-thirds scale.

When I finally tried my first landing, our director wanted to shoot it. There was no guarantee that I would be able to land, and if I did, there was no guarantee that I would be able to take off again. We needed to get whatever footage we could right from the first landing attempt.

I flew up the little valley in the opposite direction I would use for landing. When I passed the hovering helicopter camera ship, I made a steep bank around it and started to let down into the narrow channel through the trees. When 56 and I got down between the trees, the strong quartering headwind was cut off and we began to settle more than I had anticipated. I did not dare accelerate for fear I would overshoot. Instead, I pulled back on the control stick and used my tiny bit of extra speed to barely keep my right wing from hitting the top of the last major tree before we broke back out into the river channel. When that happened, I started my slip to the left just like I had seen Dad do. At the same instant, the wind that had been blocked by the trees hit us again. It looked like my slide to the left was going to take me past the end of the beach and into the trees on the far side of the river.

I had already tried the approach with the helicopter a couple of times. The helicopter was using a lot of power to hover. I knew his fuel had to be getting low so I figured it was time 56 and I took our best shot at making a landing. I lowered my right wing just a little bit to arrest my left slide, and crossed the end of the beach like that. With adrenaline pumping and every nerve tight with anticipation, I felt a strange mixture of fear and excitement. Somehow I felt like I was coming home. My right wheel brushed the sand and I used it to help stop my slide toward the river. Before I even reached the dogleg in the beach, I knew I was going to make it. Just before I slowed to a stop, I heard Martina give the victory whoop over the helicopter radio: "Okay, now swing your tail around while we still have the shot." I could tell from the excitement in her voice that she was getting the footage she had been hoping for.

The shot was in the can. I taxied back down to where Barry and our aerial unit director, Tom, were waiting for me. Tom came running up as the prop made its last few swings and came to a stop. He grabbed me as I jumped out of good old *56 Henry*. As he held me at arm's length, his face was full of emotion.

"You told me how much you wished you could have been there to see your dad land on Palm Beach, remember? Well, you just got something better. You got to land on Palm Beach." *Wow!* Tom was right. I had been concentrating so hard on landing on that tiny beach without either hurting or killing myself and *56 Henry* that I had not even thought about how incredibly unlikely this was. Millions of people would soon witness the recreation of my dad's landing, an event that eloquently symbolized the risk and drama those five men subjected themselves to in order to reach the Waodani. And not only would I be there to watch it happen, I would be taking Dad's place at the controls.

God does not promise that all of life's chapters will be easy. He does promise, however, that in the last chapter He will finally make sense of all the others. Landing on "Palm Beach" in *End of the Spear* was like a soothing salve on an open wound. I could see God's hands all over this very special sand castle in my life.

As incredible as it was for me to recreate my dad's flying in *End of the Spear*, my mom experienced something even more poignant with the new *56 Henry*. Ginny and I were flying the little yellow plane back to our home after the final alterations had finally been made to it for the filming of *End of the Spear*. As we crossed the border into Florida, Ginny commented that we had not seen Mom in quite a while even though she just lived an hour north of us. I told Ginny it would not be hard to deviate over to a little airport in Keystone Heights, where Mom was living in a little retirement center.

I called Mom on my cell phone from the plane.

Mom answered and was excited about the possibility of having Ginny and me stop by on our flight south. I thought Mom knew we were flying *56 Henry* home. She didn't.

When we landed and taxied up to the parking area, I saw Mom standing by the chain-link fence. She looked almost like a little girl as she leaned on the fence, her fingers holding on to the wire on both sides of her head. I taxied up to the fence and swung the tail as I cut the engine. As I walked over to the fence, Mom's face was glowing. But she was looking at me, not at *56 Henry*. Then I saw her focus go back to the plane, watching for Ginny.

That is when it happened. Mom finally saw what she had thought she would never see again. That little plane that had taxied out of our yard almost a half century earlier, taking her handsome husband away for the last time, had come back. The pilot was about twenty-five years older this time, and some of his features resembled Mom's more than Dad's, but that did not dampen the surprise of recognition on Mom's face.

I took Mom for a ride in *56 Henry Jr.* It was as if we had been transported back in time even though we were flying over Florida scrub rather than Amazon rain forest. Mom looked at me and smiled. For just an instant, I saw a much younger woman in the plane with me, full of anticipation, love, and the joy of life in its prime. I glimpsed a faraway look in Mom's eyes, and I think for just an instant, she saw someone else sitting in the pilot seat too. I wish I could have been the man I think she saw, even if just for a minute.

As Ginny and I taxied out to take off for home, I could almost hear Mom saying, "I wondered if I would ever see that little airplane taxi out again." Only now, at the end of her earthly life, she finally had.

Never say never, when God is writing your story!

+

+

CHAPTER 13

SAND CASTLE UNDER CONSTRUCTION

Ginny and I recently watched a movie titled *Glory Road*. It was an inspiring story about a small Texas school basketball team that took the NCAA championship away from powerhouse Kentucky in 1966. Not only was the team from El Paso a huge underdog, it was also controversial. Their coach, who had been coaching a girls team at another no-name school, ignored the unspoken rule to include only a token "Negro" on the team.

This coach wanted to win but did not have the money or school prestige necessary to recruit a winning team. So he chose great players other white schools would not play. In the final game, after threats and abuse, the coach got fed up and decided to use only his black players. He wanted to prove to the arrogant and bigoted crowd that black players were just as good and just as deserving as white players. And, no surprise, they won. I actually thought they might just barely lose. The movie was almost too good to follow the traditional win-against-all-odds story line.

With formula movies, you know what is going to happen right from the outset. Underdogs fight against poverty, physical handicaps, misunderstandings—and they triumph. Movies like that succeed because we imagine ourselves on that Texas Western College team, just like we picture ourselves on Denzel Washington's football team or in the Space Age chariot race in *Star Wars: The Phantom Menace.* Good triumphs over evil, and we are on the winning team as we walk into the sunset to live happily ever after.

But God's sand castles are not just formula structures where we win and live happily ever after. Some are like that. But most follow a different formula. They are often places where in spite of pain, insults, animosity, cruelty, and discrimination, we have an unexplainable sense of peace and well-being because we know God has a plan and we know we are part of it. And the result of real sand castles is that we know we aren't alone even if we seem to be. The structures on your life's shoreline prove that Someone else is on your beach—Someone who has a design.

In both the formula movie and the building of a sand castle, there is a time when we don't know what the outcome will be. We have to exercise faith and hope until the scene changes and we see clearly that God does exist and that He cares.

The aspect of faith is so important to the making of a sand castle that I wanted to include one chapter in this book that doesn't yet have an ending. This is a sand castle still in the making.

When Mart Green, a total stranger from Oklahoma City, called me out of the clear blue and told me he wanted to make a movie of my story, I was immediately leery. I don't consider it "my story." God wrote the story; I just had a front-row seat.

Half a lifetime ago, I learned the secret to avoiding trouble in life: Never attempt, never fail. I like to play it safe, and often that means not playing at all. When Mart called, my first thought was, *Don't play, don't get hurt.*

I told Mart that before I would even consider his offer, he needed to ask the Waodani, and I assumed that would surely be the end of the discussion. But Mart surprised me, traveling with me to Ecuador, where he convinced the Waodani to share their story. Once they said yes, then what could I say?

The more I got to know Mart and his team, the more I respected him, and I realized that, as long as the potential benefits continued to far outweigh the potential risks, I should help make the movie a reality. I feel responsible to be a good steward of this story.

My role was to give the film team access to the story. As they researched, they realized that it involved the lives and substories of a lot of different people. There were the five men killed in the story, the five widows, the nine children, my real aunt, the missionaries on the search party, the *Time Life* photographer, and numerous significant players on the Waodani side of the story.

It was not like I could just tell Mart to ask someone else for help. I knew all the key players in the story. My family and I had lived among the Waodani, and I could communicate with them. I had a history with their tribe that went back to the first gift exchange. Right before filming began in Panama, Mart gave me another call just as unanticipated as his first. From the tone of his voice, I thought that something terrible had happened. Perhaps someone had been killed, or at the very least, the movie project was shut down.

Nope, no one was dead, and the movie was still tentatively ready to start. But Mart had some news that was painful, both for him to deliver and for me to receive. He had just discovered that Chad Allen, the actor who had been offered the contract to play my dad's role—and mine—was an open homosexual.

My initial reaction was not against Mart, or even Chad, whom I knew nothing about except that he had been part of the *Dr. Quinn, Medicine Woman* cast. My first thought was, *Oh no, here we go again. Life has dealt us another card that will be tricky to play.*

This definitely seemed to be a no-win situation. Dealing with the idea that my precious memories of my dad, the first hero in my life, were now going to be sullied by this situation was a blow. With very few exceptions, everything I had ever heard about my dad was extraordinary. That is part of the mystique of being a martyr and a hero of the faith.

Having Chad, an open homosexual, play the part of my dad in the movie was terribly emotional for me. It had little to do with Chad, actually. The issue was that I wanted a "Nate Saint" to play Nate Saint. As it turns out, I wasn't the only one. And I knew that I had to decide what to do about this.

"How was Chad cast for the part?" I asked Mart, who described the process to me. Mark, the casting director, had interviewed actors for all the major parts. He is a professional, and he did not cast actors based on their personal lives. He was looking for actors who could play the "hypocrite"—that's right, acting is the art of hypocrisy, one person pretending to be someone else.

"Chad stood out from anyone else who wanted to play the part of Nate," the casting director told Mart. "Even if you wanted to establish a moral grid through which to screen actors, the Screen Actors Guild and discrimination laws would not allow it. You told me you wanted to make a good movie—one with a good script that was true to the story and had good acting that the audience would believe."

Chad had been the best one to play Dad's part. Besides, the casting director told us that Chad loved the story. He had told the casting director that he was drawn to it and that even if he wasn't given an acting role, he was interested in working on the project in some other capacity. Mark offered him the part.

On the telephone, Mart started to explain what our options were. I could tell he felt terrible about the situation.

"I've already asked Mark if we could get out of the contract. I did not want you to have to deal with this, Steve," he said. "I told you that I would do everything possible to be sensitive to the Waodani and to the families, and then I let this happen."

But while Mart was talking, I was thinking, *How would Dad feel about this?* It occurred to me that I already had a good clue. Dad knew that there were people who would be upset about what he and the other four men were attempting to do when they contacted the "Aucas." In fact, Dad even addressed some of that criticism in a letter he wrote just twenty-one days before his death: "As we weigh the future and seek the will of God, does it seem right that we should hazard our lives for just a few savages?"

Dad, Ed, Jim, Pete, and Roger did not risk their lives for mothers and children trapped in burning buildings. Their last act was not the stuff that the majority of our culture would even respect now. They certainly would not be made heroes for such a gamble. They risked leaving behind widows and fatherless children with only the chance that they might break a trail of hope into a culture of death and hatred.

"As we have a high old time this Christmas, may we who know Christ hear the cry of the damned as they hurtle headlong into the Christless night without ever a chance," Dad wrote in his last Christmas letter. Back in 1956, he knew that he and his partners were going to face criticism for what they were about to do. There were only two choices open to them: Turn their backs on the physical and spiritual plight of these "savage nomads," or do something to help them. There was significant risk either way.

Dad did not ask to be part of one of the most compelling missionary stories of the twentieth century. I did not ask for a movie to be made, nor did I make it easy for Mart Green to get in the door.

Dad did not choose to have the "Aucas" living on his doorstep, where he simply could not ignore their presence or plight. I did not choose Chad Allen to play my dad's part in the movie. I also did not know Chad had grown up with a sexual attraction for other boys. I was no more responsible for Chad's situation than Dad was responsible for the Waodani's egalitarian, violent society.

None of that had changed with Mart's painful telephone call. What changed was that I now had to deal with the state of affairs as it actually existed, not as I would have liked it to be.

Mart was willing to pay Chad and not use him. He wanted to break the contract, but we both knew there is no honorable way to do a dishonorable thing. The very reason that I had finally agreed to help Mart make *End of the Spear* was that I profoundly trusted him. I believed he would never break his word to me. I could not—no, I would not ask him to break his word to another man.

Finally, it seemed that the only way we could keep Chad from acting in *End of the Spear* was for me to ask him to voluntarily step down. That I was willing to do—at first.

There were only two details holding me back from invoking this solution. First, I did not think it was what my dad would have done. If Dad was willing to risk his life "for just a few savages," I was pretty sure he would have risked his reputation for one homosexual. The second hesitation I had was similar to the first. I don't wear a bracelet, but I couldn't help but wonder, *What would Jesus do?*

I didn't have to wonder. I already knew the answer to that one. Jesus didn't hang out with only those who seemed to be sinless. He hung out with a bunch of nobodies who were uneducated and untrained (see Acts 4:13). The few "good" and "important" guys who would even risk being associated with Jesus broke off their fledgling relationship because Jesus hung out with corrupt tax gatherers (see Mark 2:15-16). Jesus allowed an obviously immoral woman to touch Him and wash His feet (see Luke 7:36-50). He knew who she was and what she was, but Jesus was obviously more interested in what people could become than in what they had done. He spoke with compassion to the scandalous woman who had been married multiple times and was living with someone she wasn't married to (see John 4:7-29). And He turned away the mob that was planning to stone an adulteress. He didn't even give her a lecture; He simply said, don't do that anymore (see John 8:3-11).

When the news about Chad was revealed, I was already down in Panama, reassembling the replica of *56 Henry*, Dad's plane. Chad was ready to get on a plane for Panama in the next couple of days. If I was going to ask him to step down, I had to do it soon.

It is a good thing I'm just a sheep instead of the Shepherd. My instincts for mercy aren't very good. I'm much better at self-preservation. If I were shepherding one hundred sheep and one little mutton chop got lost, I would think, *Rats, one down. Wonder where he is. Maybe he'll come back; maybe I counted wrong. Can't risk the whole flock in hopes of finding just one. Guess the price of mutton and wool will have to go up a bit this year.*

In life, you win some and you lose some. But I couldn't help but think about an incident that had occurred on my trip down to Panama. I was seated on the plane next to a couple from Southern California, and we struck up a conversation. He was a doctor of Panamanian origin who had been in medical practice in the United States for years. He wanted to know why I was visiting Panama, so I told him about *End of the Spear.*

"We love movies," the doctor told me. "Who are the actors going to be?" The only one I knew anything about was Chad, but at the time, I could not even remember his last name.

"One actor's name is Chad," I said, apologizing for not having any more information on him.

"Not Chad Allen, by any chance?" the doctor had asked.

I was sure not. What are the chances that this doctor would actually know one of the actors in *End of the Spear?*

"What movies has he been in?" the doctor asked.

"I don't know. I heard he was in *Doctor Quinn, Medicine Woman.*"

"Yeah, that's him." The doctor and his wife began telling me about Chad, who had actually grown up in their neighborhood in Southern California. They had followed his career and then had lost track of him. To them, he was not just an actor; he was a real person.

I continued to replay this conversation as I drifted off to sleep that night in Panama, still struggling with how I was going to tell Chad that I wanted him to step down.

I knew we had to get this settled. I could not afford to have my mind wander while I was flying a 1940s vintage plane covered with cloth, in tight formation with a jet-powered helicopter. I knew that if I let my thoughts get cluttered with other matters there was a good chance I was going to kill myself and possibly others.

I can't explain the physiology that stimulates our minds to playact life situations in our sleep. My guess is that dreams are part of the process we use to work out solutions to problems in life that we can't afford to risk thinking about when we are awake.

I had already woken up, but I must have drifted back to a light sleep. Not quite dreaming, but definitely not fully awake, I now pictured myself being chased by a mob of angry people who were throwing things and yelling at me. I wasn't sure what they were upset about, but it was clear that I was their intended victim. Finally someone angrily yelled something like, "You'd better ask him to quit!"

I yelled back, "I will, I will!"

Then suddenly the scene changed. I was standing in a huge hall right out of *The Lord of the Rings*, and I was being interrogated. It was God. I could hear His expression more than see it. I knew instinctively that the subject was my role in the Chad Allen situation. God started His question with something like, "You, Steve Saint, of all people . . ." Here, I guess my mind was reliving the feeling I had when I got in trouble with my grade school teachers. "You of all people should know that I love all of My children. I have gone out of My way to orchestrate a situation in which My child [I knew Chad was the child God was referring to] would have the opportunity to see what it really means to follow Me, to submit his will to Mine." The expression on His face became hard, and I could sense it in His voice. "Why did you mess with My plans?"

I was awake again—fully now. And I knew what I would *not* do. I would not ask Chad Allen to step down. I also knew that I would probably pay a price for my decision. And I have.

The potential reward? I'll leave that to God. My decision was simply based on this: I would rather face the wrath of God's people here than take the chance on facing the wrath of God—or worse yet, His disappointment in me—later on.

At this point, I still had not met Chad Allen. I discussed my decision with Ginny, who told me how strongly our three sons felt about the matter. They did not want Chad playing my part. I had not thought through that yet. I realized that even though my mind was made up, this needed to be a family decision. I let Ginny and our three sons and their wives know that if any of them still wanted Chad off the project, I would ask him to step down.

I didn't want to pressure Shaun, Jaime, and Jesse into agreeing with me, so I asked Mart to explain to my family how Chad had been chosen, and how his agent had been opposed to him acting in *End of the Spear*.

In the end, everyone agreed—independently of one another—that treating Chad like Jesus would have was more important than the way we would be treated by those who disagreed with our decision.

I also discussed the situation with Mom. I could almost see

the energy physically drain out of her eighty-year-old body. She looked sad, but she said, "I may not be able to go see the movie because of this, but I think this is the decision that would most honor God. I agree."

I wrote Chad a long letter, explaining what a difficult situation we found ourselves in. In part, the letter said,

> Chad, I could not possibly relate adequately all the soul-searching and discussion and wrestling and praying that my family and I have gone through these last days, trying to decide whether we should ask you to withdraw from playing my dad (and me) in [*End of the Spear*]. We have considered doing that. . . . The purpose of this letter is to let you hear from me, as a representative of my family, that this is a painful dilemma for us. On the one hand, we cannot imagine that this won't be a lightning rod for controversy that could envelop both you and ourselves. On the other hand, we have been praying for you since before we even knew who you would be. We affirm you as a son whom God loves as dearly as any of us. We also know that the road of ease and comfort seldom leads to a significant destination. We have seen God bring good from pain, over and over and over again. That is the heart of the story you have come to be a part of. God took what appeared to be tragedy and made it a centerpiece example of what He can do with the lives of fallible men when given the authority to do so.

Chad was given my letter as soon as he arrived in Panama for filming. I went down to the beautiful lobby of the Hotel Melia to meet Chad and the actors who were going to play the parts of the other four men. Chad wasn't as tall as Dad or I, but his coloring was similar. He was articulate, but I think he was scared, too. He was probably afraid that he would be held at arm's length or openly ostracized. But he was human, a child of God. He could have been my son.

My personality tends to make me see life in black and white: too much law and far too little grace. Ready, shoot, aim. I see homosexuality as a cut-and-dried issue. It is unnatural, a perversion, and it threatens the historic fabric of our country. But that is of no consequence, really. More important than my own opinions is that God says it is wrong. Homosexuality goes against God's plan just like fornication, adultery, divorce, lust, murder, greed, lies, and gossip. Even calling someone a fool is enough for God to hand us a "life sentence" (see Matthew 5:22, NIV).

Since deciding not to ask Chad to step down from playing Dad's role, I have heard some clever defenses for my decision. Movie director Jim Hanon had a good one: "This is a 'bucket drop' to the homosexual community"; just like the gift drops to the Waodani opened the door for a relationship with them, Chad could give us an opportunity to minister to people who need Jesus. The door between hurting people in the homosexual community and most conservative Christians is almost as tightly shut as the door between the Waodani and the outside world was when five men gave their lives to crack it open.

My involvement forced me to do some deep evaluation of what my role as a God follower should be to immoral, degenerate, unrepentant, God-mocking people around me. Paul says that I shouldn't have anything to do with immoral people. No, no, wait. I got that wrong. He says, "I have written you in my letter not to associate with sexually immoral people—not at all meaning the people of this world who are immoral, or the greedy and swindlers, or idolaters. In that case, you would have to leave this world" (1 Corinthians 5:9-10, NIV).

And then he goes on, "But now I am writing you that you must not associate with anyone who calls himself a brother but is sexually immoral or greedy, an idolater or a slanderer, a drunkard or a swindler. With such a man, do not even eat" (verse 11).

God followers are not supposed to be separate from the world; we are supposed to be in the world, but not of it. The problem is not having the boat in the water; it is having water in the boat. There never was a danger in making *End of the Spear* that Nate Saint might be influenced to live like Chad Allen. But there was a chance Chad Allen might—by God's grace and strength and the kind understanding of His people—have been influenced to live like Nate Saint.

During the filming, Chad and I talked right after he finished the spearing scene where my father was killed. It was an emotional scene, difficult for him to act, and even more difficult for me to watch. As soon as the last scene had been shot, Chad turned to me and asked, "What is sin?" Sin is such a tough concept, and I didn't want to use platitudes or sixteenth-century language, so I just borrowed Mincaye's explanation.

"Mincaye would say, 'Doing badly is those things that *Waengongi* does not see well that we do and those things *Waengongi* sees well that we don't do.'"

I'm still praying for Chad, and I'm praying for myself, too. *Waengongi* has cleaned my heart so that it is clear like the sky with no clouds in it. But there are always clouds on the horizon, and there is a lot of mud being slung around down here.

Because of my decision, one of my dearest friends has not spoken to me in a couple of years. He has publicly denounced my character, my integrity, and my veracity. An activist pastor went on the air and claimed that I said some things to *Advocate Magazine* that I simply did not say. In fact, I didn't even know the magazine existed until I heard his broadcast. I'm pretty sure that the Book that pastor claims as his only rule of faith and conduct also says something about verifying facts and getting both sides of a story before making up your mind about which side to take. But then, I have been guilty of that too.

I am not a proponent of homosexual rights. I don't promote the homosexual lifestyle. And I am not a homosexual. All of these have been hinted at, but they are all false. Unlike some other Christians I know, I have never had to resist homosexual urges, either. I have enough other issues to deal with, and I live every day with the knowledge that it is only by God's grace that many of the comments made about me are not true.

This controversy has changed two things related to my own perception of homosexuality. I no longer find homosexuals disgusting. I realize now that they are real people who can only live up to God's standard if they ask for and receive His help. I also realize that my feelings on this issue don't make any difference at all. The issue is not what *I* think about homosexuality, or gossip, for that matter. What matters is what *Waengongi* thinks about it.

What do you think? This has all the makings of a sand castle, and I believe that it will be. God often seems to show up just when we need Him most. I know He cares, and I'm waiting with anticipation to see how this might end. I don't know why God saw fit to have Chad play my dad in the movie. I know there are those who would detest my even suggesting that it might have been God's will. I can only say that I believe this was the trail God marked.

Many God followers were critical of my dad and his friends when they were killed too. I believe that God marked that trail as well. The difference between these two incidents is that God's plan in the first one has begun to make sense.

+

+

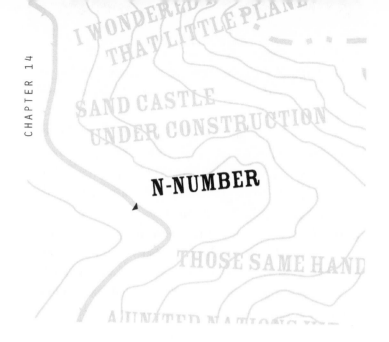

CHAPTER 14

N-NUMBER

The night before I'm going to test-fly a never-before-flown experimental plane, I usually don't sleep very well. There are a hundred things that can go wrong the first time an airplane, especially one that has been built in the garage, shrugs off the invisible bonds that tie it to earth and roars into the sky.

In one particular case, I wasn't ready to test-fly the plane yet. It had to be rebuilt first. But I was still very excited. It was a World War II vintage plane that was going to play an important role in *End of the Spear.* Since the story depicted in the movie is true, the replica plane had to be authentic. Nowhere in technological life are there more rules than in aviation. If your plane is certified with one kind of switch, you have to get special permission to substitute a better switch. An engine certified for a bunch of other planes can't be used on your plane unless it has been specifically certified for your plane.

In rebuilding the old movie plane, we had to do some

hunting around for parts. We had to improvise a few times and then fill out the proper forms to get field approval for the upgrades that needed to be made.

We spent a lot of time looking for aircraft-approved interior fabric that would match the interior color of the original plane. Nothing seemed to match the color in the picture we had of the inside of the plane. Finally it occurred to me that there were deep shadows in that picture. It must have been taken in the late jungle afternoon as the sun was setting. In the picture, the plane was sitting on a little sandbar in the headwaters of the Amazon River, so the humidity in the air would have been extreme. Such high humidity makes the light what photographers call warm. That high humidity creates the gorgeous orange and red sunsets in the tropics.

We set up some lights to simulate a late-afternoon sun in humid Florida, and bingo, we already had the right color for the interior. We just had to see it in the proper light to realize that it was our match.

After spending an incredible amount of time poring over authentic pictures and documents from the original plane, searching for parts, and then meticulously rebuilding the movie plane, I realized I had overlooked one huge detail: the N-Number.

Every plane has an N-Number assigned to it as registration identification. In the United States, it is called an N-Number because every aircraft registration begins with the letter *N*. It is usually followed by four numbers and ends with another letter. For instance, the little Piper Cub that I learned to fly in was registered as N6903H. The plane that we were rebuilding to replicate the plane in the movie was registered as N4225H. But the plane in the real story had been N5156H. If registration numbers were merely recorded in the plane's documents, it would have been no big deal. But N-Numbers have to be marked on the airplane in specified, prominent locations in large numerals and letters that can be read from another airplane or from the ground.

The plane in the story had been known by people all over the Ecuadorean jungle as *56 Henry*. Besides that, N5156H had been painted in bold black over a bright yellow background on both sides of the tail, on top of the right wing, and under the left wing. The numbers and letters were so big they looked like a flying billboard. To be authentic, I realized we would have to use the real N-Number.

The obvious, easy solution was to simply use the original plane's N-Number temporarily until the movie was shot. But that would not work because the stunt plane had to actually fly in the movie. The director wanted every flying scene to be the real deal: No computer-generated graphics in this movie, please. And it's not a good idea to fly a plane with a fake registration unless you like to spend long periods of time in solitude and eat institutional food three times a day. The easy solution was not an option.

I thought that maybe we could just superimpose the N5156H over the N4225H in the editing process after the movie was shot. But after talking to the producer, I realized this option would probably cost more than the plane itself, and I knew that the replica *56 Henry* was going to be a pretty hefty investment. Adding all the edit suite time necessary to erase all the markings on the stunt plane and replace them would make the movie plane very, very expensive—too expensive.

I would have to get the original registration, but I had no idea how to go about doing that.

I started by calling the Federal Aviation Administration offices in Oklahoma City. When I gave the woman the registration number I was looking for—November 5156 Hotel—she dropped off the line for a minute.

"That registration was issued to a plane that was destroyed in an accident or something in South America," she said when she returned. "When the plane was destroyed, the registration was withdrawn." That part of the story I already knew.

"Do you still have that N-Number available?"

"No, it was reissued to a Cessna 172 based in Salem, Oregon. It belongs to a flying club there named . . ." She droned on, but my mind was elsewhere.

Why did the new N5156H have to be owned by a club, for goodness' sake?

It seemed useless to even try to get the number. But I had no other options. I did a little investigative work, using the name and address given to me by the woman at the FAA, and I learned that the flying club president was a woman named Joan.

What I needed was a good opening line. I simply could not think of anything to say to a total stranger twenty-five hundred miles away—I needed to say something that would keep her from hanging up the phone on me. If I offended her or sounded like a crackpot, it would be easy to close the door forever. When it comes to airplanes, people just don't ask other people to trade N-Numbers; it would be similar to asking someone to trade social security numbers or names. In fact, the N-Number of the plane you fly becomes your identity every time you fly that plane. It is a very personal thing.

I can still remember the N-Number of every airplane I have ever owned. Those flying club members would think it was rude and presumptuous of me to ask them to give up their registration number. Besides that, their plane would have to be repainted, which would be an expensive inconvenience.

But maybe, I thought, *if the paint is in bad condition, I can use that to talk them out of their N-Number.* "How would you like your plane to be repainted for free?" But then I remembered that I didn't have an extra ten or fifteen thousand dollars to do that.

Finally, Ginny pushed me to just make the call.

"You keep telling me about all the little miracles God has been doing to keep this project going. There is nothing you can really do to make the N-Number happen. See what God might do about it."

Yeah, I'll bet Moses had gotten similar advice on the shore of the Red Sea.

But I couldn't think of anything else to do, so I dialed Joan's number in Salem, three-hours-behind-Florida, Oregon. The receptionist answered and told me Joan was out of the office.

"Can you tell me what this concerns, and would you like me to have her return your call?"

"No, I mean, yes . . ." I stammered. I didn't want to sound like a telephone solicitor. But if I left my number, she would see that I lived in Florida, where she probably didn't know anyone. Her guard would be up, and I would have lost the element of surprise. On the other hand, maybe that was best.

"I could leave my number," I said, "but if you tell me when you expect her back, I'll try once more, and if she's not in then, I'll leave my number so she can call me back." Whew, it sounded kind of normal—I hoped.

This was like taking the stand in a trial. It is no big deal until it is your turn. Then your mind races over all the instructions your attorney has given you: Act assured but not anxious. Sit comfortably, but don't look bored. Answer the question, but don't give any additional information.

I called back later, and the receptionist put me through to Joan.

"This is Joan. How may I help you?" *Oh boy, here we go.*

"Hi, Joan, this is Steve Saint, and I'm calling from Florida. You don't know me, but . . ."

She cut me off. Boy did this look like it was going to be a short conversation. I expected her next sentence to be: "Look, Mr. Saint, is it? I appreciate your taking your valuable time to call me, but we don't accept telephone solicitations. Please save us both some time and call someone else so I can get back to work."

But Joan went in a different direction. "Steve Saint? Are you by any chance Nate Saint's son?" Three hundred million people live between Joan in Oregon and me in Florida. And she knew my dad?

"Yes, ma'am, I am."

"Really? Well, do you have a minute for me to tell you a story?"

Oh please, I thought, *tell me all of your stories. Take all day. I'm in no rush, because when you finish saying whatever it is that you have to say to me, I am going to have to ask you for a very personal favor, and you are going to answer no, and I don't want to get to that point, and if you take some of my time, maybe you won't care if I do ask my personal favor—at least not quite as much.*

"Sure, go ahead." I hoped that I sounded interested but not anxious.

Joan proceeded to tell me an incredible story. "Well, when my sister and I were young, my parents read about your father.

They wanted to be missionaries after that, but it never worked out. We did start a tradition, though. Every year they would read us a book titled *Through Gates of Splendor*. Are you familiar with that book?"

"Yes, ma'am, I am," I said. Aunt Betty had written that book, and six chapters of it were taken almost directly from my dad's journals. *I guess I am familiar with it,* I thought.

"Well, I got interested in flying and got my license. And my husband is a pilot too. In fact, we have a flying club."

The story was starting to get interesting. *Keep talking, Joan. Just crack the door ever so slightly and give me a teeny, tiny opening to ask you for your N-Number—pleeeeease!*

"Every time someone joins our club, I have them over for dinner. Then I loan them my copy of that book as an unobtrusive way of sharing my faith with them. If you like planes, you almost have to like that book."

This was great. Joan needed a copy of my dad's biography, *Jungle Pilot*. Pilots would really like that book too. Maybe I would send her a copy, along with some other mementos, and then when things warmed up, I would ask for her N-Number.

"Ten days ago," she continued, "we had a member of our club over for dinner, and I loaned him the book. While I was fixing dinner, he started looking at the pictures, and all of a sudden he said the most incredible thing: 'Hey, Joan, did you know that the plane in this book has our N-Number on it?'

"Well, I knew that couldn't be, but he was insistent, so I went over to look at the picture. Sure enough, your dad's plane had our N-Number on it. Or, rather, we have your dad's N-Number on one of our club planes."

Wow. I had procrastinated for weeks before calling Joan, trying to figure out how to let her know who I was and why I needed her N-Number. Now, almost fifty years after Dad and his plane had disappeared from my life, this total stranger was telling me that she knew that story and that it had defined much of her life!

I realized that I didn't need a clever opening line or a spellbinding story to connect with Joan. I only needed to tell her my name.

Joan continued her story. "I couldn't believe the incredible coincidence that our plane shared an N-Number with your dad's, so I called my sister and told her about it.

"'Joan, you think *that* is a coincidence?' she said. 'Last night I went to a Steven Curtis Chapman concert. A short time into the concert Steve asked the audience if we wanted to go on an adventure with him to the Amazon jungle.'"

I knew where this story was going. Mincaye and I had been at that concert as a part of Steve's sixty-five-city tour. After opening the concert, Steve would ask the audience if they wanted to take a journey with him to the Amazon. Then, as he and his band sang songs—several of them written specifically about this story—a giant movie screen behind the stage told the story God had written us into. After about thirty-five minutes, Steve would say something like, "I would like to tell you more about this story, but there is someone with us tonight who knows the story much better than I do."

At that point he would introduce me, and I would walk out onstage. We had done it night after night, but the audience's reaction always amazed me. People would gasp, often putting their hands up to their faces like I was a ghost or something. I think a lot of people had probably heard something of this story but thought it happened back in David Livingstone's time rather than in their lifetime. I usually gave a synopsis of the story from my point of view, and then the *big* surprise came when I ended my talk about God's amazing intervention that made it possible for me to love and become family with Mincaye, the same man who brutally speared my father.

I would end by telling the audience, "I wish I could take all of you down to the Amazon jungle so you could meet Grandfather Mincaye and so that you could see what a kind, fun-loving, and gentle God follower he has become. But I can't do that. There are just too many of you. So Steve (Chapman) suggested that maybe I should bring Grandfather here to meet you."

At this point, I could almost see the blood drain out of people's faces. They would just sit stunned. That's when Mincaye would walk onto the stage, wearing his feathered headdress, earplugs, and pig-tooth necklace. Every time he appeared, people broke into thunderous applause in a standing ovation to God's incredible acts of transformation and reconciliation through the ages.

Joan's sister, Lois, went on, "Last night, I met the man who killed Nate Saint, and I met Nate's son Steve!"

Joan asked her, "You don't know if Nate's son is also a pilot, do you?"

Lois answered, "Yeah, they showed him flying down in the jungles in the concert video last night."

Now Joan addressed me directly. "I thought to myself, *I'll bet Steve wants his dad's N-Number.* So Lois and I decided to try to find a way to get in touch with you, and here you are, calling me instead! You want that N-Number, don't you?"

Dad was gone and his plane was gone. I had never once, in almost half a century, wondered what had happened to that N-Number—until it was needed for the making of *End of the Spear.*

If I had waited a couple of days to make my call, Joan probably would have found my number and called me. But this way was much more dramatic.

Coincidences do happen. But calling this a coincidence would really be a stretch. It was a whole lot easier to believe that this was dramatic evidence of God's intervention in the retelling of His story, and proof that He cares about even the little affairs in our lives.

While you decide what you believe about this, I'm going to mosey out to the airport and take *56 Henry* up for a spin.

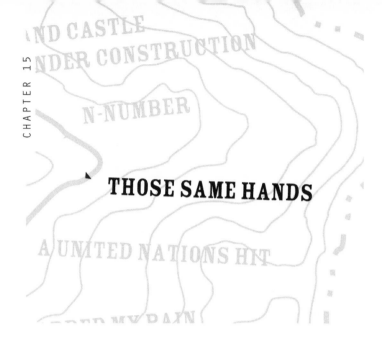

CHAPTER 15

THOSE SAME HANDS

The people who speared my father to death when I was a boy asked me to return to the Amazon jungle to live with them as a man. Masters of their own world, they wanted to learn skills from the outside world that would enable them to care for their own needs and the needs of their people.

Joining the Space Age with the Stone Age is not easy—with two-way radios for telephones and the Amazon grocery's meat department running wild, there were major adjustments to be made on both sides in this experiment.

But Grandfather Mincaye and the Waodani God followers treated me like family. They wanted to help their people physically and spiritually, and they wanted me to help them help their people.

When the Waodani first told me they wanted to learn to practice dentistry, I mistakenly filed their assertions in my mental file I use for kids labeled, "When I grow up I'm going to be a . . ."

How could they learn to fix teeth and treat infections? Some of them were old enough to have great-grandchildren. And these people had little or no education. Only one of them knew how to read. Most of the others didn't even know the alphabet. They could count to twenty on their fingers and toes, but they didn't do math; and they wanted to do dental work? I didn't think this would work. But I realized they wanted to do it to help others, so I patronizingly thought, *Isn't that sweet?*

But my jungle family really wanted to learn to fix teeth, and they were persistent. Several of them had become quite expert at extracting teeth. Although they did not have adequate equipment or access to anesthesia, they made it very clear to me that they wanted the tools and training to help them take care of their people's dental needs.

"First we will take care of our people's teeth, and then while we are fixing their teeth, we will teach them how *Waengongi*— the Creator—can fix their hearts so they can live forever," they said.

"Don't God's carvings say that all God followers should teach others to walk His trail?" they asked. I had to agree. Jesus Himself told us to make disciples everywhere. Then we're told to teach these disciples everything we have been taught (see 2 Timothy 2:2).

The great commission is a relay race. Jesus ran the first lap. He taught His disciples, then He taught them to teach their disciples, and now it is our turn to teach ours. Christ commissioned us to run our laps. But the race isn't done until we hand the baton off to others. According to John 15:8, the proof that we are doing the job Jesus gave us is when our disciples start bearing fruit themselves.

Okay, so my illiterate jungle family wanted to learn to fix teeth for their people, and then they wanted to teach people in other places to fix other people's teeth. Finally, they wanted to share the Good News of Christ with those they were helping. I tried to imagine one of these old jungle warriors in China or India. That was a stretch.

But over the next few years, we experimented with off-the-shelf dental equipment that we stripped down to its bare essentials. It worked, but it was difficult to get it to run in places where we had to generate our own electricity with gasoline and oil that had to be flown in by plane. And it was extremely difficult to keep the equipment running. Dental supply companies don't usually think about ways to keep giant jungle thorns from ripping holes in the pneumatic lines that power their drills and suction equipment. Most of their clients don't have dirt floors, 100 percent humidity, and wildly fluctuating electrical voltages. We did!

Finally it became evident that we would have to reinvent our dental equipment from scratch. That took several years, but with Darrell, our persistent, highly qualified designer at the helm, we finally got the job done. The subassemblies are made in China and then shipped to our I-TEC (Indigenous People's Technology and Education Center) for final assembly and shipping.

Next we had to reinvent the way training would be done. Many of our early "lay dental practitioners" could not read. Most of those we wanted to teach did not speak a language we understood. So we decided we would make our training system nonverbal. We would teach by demonstration and nonverbal communication only. That way we could go anywhere in the world and teach anyone with basic dexterity and a desire to learn.

Sure enough, just like the Waodani had dreamed, we started receiving requests to do dental training in South America, Africa, China, and even India. When the request came from India, we found that they had heard about God followers in Africa learning to do dentistry using I-TEC dental equipment and methods. The Africans had heard about the Waodani learning to care for their own people's teeth and told the people from India about it. The Indians hoping to learn dentistry wanted to show people of other faiths that they cared about them as people and not just as potential converts. But they were highly doubtful that they could actually master the skills necessary to extract and fix teeth. In addition to asking I-TEC to supply equipment and the training curriculum, they made one more unusual request.

They asked that I be part of the training team, and they asked me to bring Grandfather Mincaye to help with the actual training. We learned later that there was method to their madness. They knew that Mincaye couldn't read or write, and they were convinced that if he could do this, then they could master it too.

The problem they had not thought about was that Mincaye lives in the Amazon jungle. For him to get to India was like my going to the moon. It wasn't entirely impossible, but it was highly improbable.

When the request came, Mincaye was in the United States, where we had been doing publicity for *Beyond the Gates of Splendor* and *End of the Spear*. The United States was logistically much closer to India than Ecuador, but strategically it was just as far. Mincaye would need a visa to get into India. But being Ecuadorean, he would need to apply for his visa from Ecuador. Unfortunately, there is no Indian consulate in Ecuador. And Mincaye doesn't have mail service out in the jungle. Also, he can't fill out the necessary forms or sign them. I assumed that Mincaye and I weren't going to India, no matter how badly the Indian pastors wanted it to happen. But I forgot about the divine intervention option.

Fortunately, Brad, a colleague at I-TEC, did not forget about divine intervention. He called the Indian Embassy in Houston, where a kind woman stuck her neck out and agreed to give Mincaye a visa so he could go as part of the dental training team.

I had told Mincaye that there were people living on the opposite side of the world, and I explained that the world was round like a *paibo*—ball. He didn't buy it. He was convinced that "the world being round, then no one could live on the underside. Being there they would just fall off." Now I told Mincaye that we were going to go visit those people on the "bottom of the dirt."

"Going, we will teach them to do the 'tooth thing.'"

He just gave me his usual jovial smile. We boarded the plane in Denver, flew to Detroit, and from there flew to Amsterdam. We flew from Amsterdam all the way to Bombay (now Mumbai). By the time we got to Hyderabad, we had been traveling for about a day and a half.

My son Jaime Nate Mincaye and other members of the team were waiting for us at the airport. Mincaye looked a little dazed, but the fact that he couldn't understand what anyone was saying didn't faze him. I realized that to him, India was no different from the United States or Europe or even Ecuador, for that matter. He couldn't understand what anyone said any-where except in the comparatively tiny little piece of Amazon rain forest where his small tribe of people lives.

But that doesn't mean Mincaye can't communicate. He had us laughing before we left the terminal, pantomiming about how hard it was not to be able to go to the bathroom for thirteen hours and how the woman on the plane tried to get us to do finger exercises and leg stretches and other strange contortions.

The dental training team was headed up by Charlie, a den-tist from Louisville, Kentucky, who had already been in Hyder-abad for a couple of days. They had already done their anatomy training and had taught the pastors to give each other shots of anesthesia. And they had learned how to set up the I-TEC portable dental systems they would be using.

As soon as we had something to eat, they were going to take us to a dental clinic in a rural area outside the bustling city. On our way out there, our host explained that some of the pastors had been severely persecuted in this area by militant members of another religion. In fact, one member of the group of pastors we were training had recently been killed for trying to share his faith.

I realized that caring for hurting peoples' physical needs was a great way to earn the right to minister to their spiritual needs. I admired the pastors we were there to train. They weren't try-ing to push their faith on anyone. They just wanted to offer their fellow Indians an opportunity to hear and understand the Good News that God loved them and had provided a way for them to "live happily in peace with Him forever," as Mincaye would say. They were even willing to suffer for the opportunity to tell others what God had done for them. But instead of suffering needlessly, they were stepping out of their comfort zones to learn skills that would allow them to meet a need and end terrible suffering for others.

When we arrived at the place where the clinic was going to be held, a crowd of people was already waiting. One of the pastors told me that when they used to come to this town, the crowd gathered to throw insults and rocks at them. "Now, they have come to let us touch them and help them." I certainly liked the second response better than the first.

It was amazing to watch these young lay dental technicians talking to their patients, evaluating and recording the dental work they needed, and then actually working on them. So far, they were just doing extractions. We would teach them to do restorations at the end of the week. The neophyte dental techs knew how to use the equipment, and they gave the impression that they had been giving shots of anesthesia for years. They were not hesitant to jump in when they knew what to do, or to ask Charlie for help when they didn't know what to do. I was watching one of the pastor teams work on a thin woman with the characteristic Hindu mark on her forehead, when they started to discuss what they should do next.

They had given the young woman anesthesia and had started the preliminary procedures to extract a badly abscessed tooth when they began their discussion. I looked over their shoulders and saw what was concerning them. It looked like the woman's tooth had been abscessing for a long time. It was difficult to tell what was tooth and what was jaw bone. Both had been severely eaten away by the infection. I have had some basic dental training, but I certainly did not know what to do in this case.

The young pastors called Charlie over to bail them out. But when Charlie took a look, he turned to me and commented,

"Man, I don't do this kind of work often. I send patients like this to an oral surgeon."

Now what to do? Everyone was clearly happy we had come. But how long they would stay happy if we broke this woman's jaw was hard to predict. I remembered the rocks and insults this village had thrown at the pastors when they saw them as uncaring proselytizers.

I was beginning to feel a little bit uncomfortable. I have a lot of experience taking people to places where they cannot speak the native language and don't know local customs. Now I found myself in the same situation. If things turned ugly I didn't know what I would do. And how could I explain to Grandfather Mincaye what was going on? Charlie was about to make my perceived dilemma worse.

"Steve, let's ask Mincaye what he would do if he was going to pull this tooth," he said. Charlie wanted the trainees to see how capable Mincaye was. I wondered if I had exaggerated Mincaye's ability. Now he would not just be a bystander I needed to get out of harm's way; he could actually be held responsible. I was very careful to explain to Grandfather that Doctor Charlie wanted to know what he *would do* if he was going to pull this woman's tooth. I didn't want him to think we actually wanted him to do it.

But Grandfather Mincaye is not into abstract ideas. He could see that this woman had a problem that had been causing her pain for a long time. No one else was taking charge, so Mincaye did.

When Mincaye bent over the patient from behind the chair, she looked like she wasn't going to need anesthesia. She had probably already been nervous having Christian pastors touching her while several foreigners looked on. But when Mincaye bent over to inspect her tooth, she didn't see him coming. He still had his feather headdress on, and his very large earlobes with big holes in them hanging down across his cheeks no doubt made him look fearsome to this already panicky woman.

Mincaye did not hesitate. He saw that the other dental technicians were using latex gloves, so he held his hands up for me to put gloves on him. He looked like Dr. Kildare getting gloved for surgery—only short, dark, with large ear holes, and with many more miles showing in his dynamic old face.

I thought he was just going to examine the patient. But I was wrong. He picked up an elevator and started working on that tooth. I held the LED headlamp for him and then helped support the woman's jaw when he started using the forceps. I was praying that the tooth would come out, both for the woman's sake and for ours. Sure enough. With one final, gentle twist, Mincaye lifted out what was left of that old tooth and placed it gently on the instrument tray.

But he wasn't done. I was holding the woman's jaw, massaging the area where Mincaye had extracted the tooth to minimize the bleeding and swelling. While I was still holding the woman's face, Mincaye placed his hands over mine and began praying for her. He prayed that *Waengongi* would not only heal her jaw but would also "clear her heart so she could see His very good trail." He had been so gentle and kind that it brought tears to my eyes to see him minister to this stranger halfway around the globe from where he had been born into a violent Stone Age society.

As I watched him pray, I looked down at his gentle hands placed over mine and realized that these were the same hands that had once driven spears through my precious father's body; these were *those same hands*. The hands that had once brutally torn my only hero from me at the age of five were now, fifty years later, holding my hands in love as we attempted to show a woman on another continent with a red dot on her forehead that Father Creator—who had changed our hearts and made us, men who should have been enemies, into family—wanted to change hers too.

As Aslan in C. S. Lewis's *The Lion, the Witch and the Wardrobe* so eloquently pronounces, "There is a magic deeper still which [the Witch] did not know. . . . When a willing victim who had committed no treachery was killed in a traitor's stead . . . Death itself would start working backward."[7]

I still remember the anguish I felt as a little boy when Mom told me my dad, my hero, was never going to come back to live with us. My little-boy universe began to come apart because all my dreams had centered on my dad. Who would have dared to guess that one day the man who killed my dad would become one of my dearest and most trusted friends? Who could have foreseen that those same hands that once were so brutal would half a century later demonstrate God's love on the opposite side of the planet? I knew, even as I watched this scene unfold, that this was a God sign.

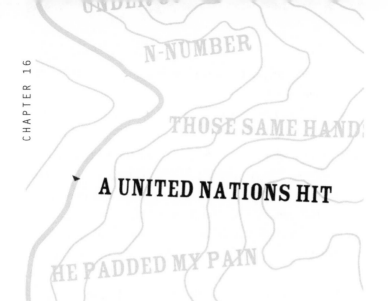

CHAPTER 16

A UNITED NATIONS HIT

I don't know a lot about the United Nations. When I was in college at the University of South Florida in Tampa, we staged a mock UN conference, and what I remember is a lot of maneuvering by student delegates to have their portfolios recognized. It was highly political but not very practical. I don't remember wrestling with real-life issues or calamities that were pitting country against country and people against people.

What I have read and heard about the actual UN makes me think that our mock United Nations was actually quite realistic. Lots of money spent, lots of talk bandied about, and enough corruption to attract a revolving door of diplomats. My reading, however, is usually from the newspaper, and I do know enough to acknowledge that what we read in newspapers and hear in news reports seldom bears close resemblance to the actual state of world affairs. I recognize that I know little about the real workings of the world body that is headquartered in the United States but has had a tumultuous affair with the U.S. government for decades.

When *End of the Spear* was released in January 2006, Mincaye and I were asked to do publicity interviews all over the country, ending in New York the day before the film's nationwide opening. On the evening before the January 20 opening, a private showing was arranged for the cast and crew, media guests, and other VIPs. Mincaye and I were there, along with the actors who had played our parts in the movie. A surprising number of other actors, along with spouses and friends, also showed up.

Mincaye and I were introduced and made brief comments before the movie. Afterward Louie Leonardo, who played "Mincayani" in the movie, and some of the other actors arranged a cast reunion party at a local restaurant. But before Ginny, Mincaye, and I could leave, we were told that some dignitaries had come to the showing and wanted to meet us. We had been meeting so many people over the past month that people and places were a blur. I had no idea who these dignitaries were. I figured we would be pleasant, answer the same questions we had already answered hundreds of times, and then be off to the party, where we would put in a short appearance before collapsing back in our midtown Manhattan hotel.

Before the dignitaries could get to us, several pushy media people cornered Mincaye and me, and I could not gracefully extricate us from the unscheduled and unappreciated domination of one particular journalist. I knew the waiting dignitaries would leave unless someone on the film team came to our rescue and informed the aggressive journalist that other people were waiting to meet us and we really had to go.

I was wrong. The dignitaries waited until everyone else had

gone and our domineering journalist ran out of comments to make and questions to ask. Then the dignitaries, all women, surrounded Mincaye and me. They were Latin, yet their enthusiasm for *End of the Spear* seemed exaggerated even by Latin standards. One of the women commented, "This is like light at the end of the tunnel; this is what we spend our lives trying to do but without success."

I really did not know what she was referring to; I didn't realize that they worked at the United Nations. Another woman from a Central American country said something like, "We keep trying to change how people act, but here the change comes about because the people's hearts are changed. That is what we need to do, change people's hearts."

Finally the woman who seemed to be in charge of the group asked me, "How can we have this movie shown at the United Nations?"

I had no say over where the movie would be shown, and I was sure this was just a grandiose gesture that would never become a reality. Just the idea of a movie controlled by Christians being shown at the United Nations seemed preposterous to me. What would Hindus, Buddhists, animists, Muslims, and atheists think about a secular organization hosting a movie with a strong religious message, especially considering that the message was Christian?

I suggested that the diplomats confer with representatives of Every Tribe Entertainment, who were in charge of distributing *End of the Spear*, and then Ginny and I were off to the cast party for what I hoped would be a brief appearance.

We had much more fun at the cast party than we had anticipated. It was really good to see friends we had worked beside and gotten to know in the Panamanian jungles while the movie was being shot. Mart Green, the executive producer, and some of his family even showed up. Mart made his way over to me and shouted over the noisy, wall-to-wall crowd that he had just been approached by several UN diplomats, who wanted him to show *End of the Spear* in the United Nations Secretariat Building: "You know, the building with all the flags out in front."

For a brief moment I thought, *Well, who knows? Stranger things have happened.* Then I just dismissed the idea. Surely everyone at the UN was too busy to give up two hours for a Christian film.

Again, I was wrong. A couple of weeks later, Mart called and said that the diplomats who had been at the January 19 showing were serious. They had recruited numerous other delegates to sponsor the showing of *End of the Spear* in the UN's own theater. They had explained to Mart that many diplomats would not want to be seen going into a commercial theater to see *End of the Spear*, but there seemed to be a growing group that wanted to see it in the security of their own office building.

A number of principal members of the movie team were also going to be there. Mart wanted me to attend to represent the real people in the story. I still couldn't believe that *End of the Spear* was actually going to be shown in the headquarters of world secularism. I doubted that it was really going to happen—show a Christian movie to United Nations diplomats, right in their own headquarters? Sure, if it *was* going to happen, I was game to go.

On the big day, we had quite an entourage from the movie team. We were given a briefing and told that there was no way to know how many diplomats would show up. To avoid the stigma of having a record of who attended, no tickets were given out. The showing would be strictly first-come, first-served. As we entered the building with multiple rows of flags out in front, we first had to go through airport-type security and then we received a leisurely tour of the secretariat building. When our guide led us toward the Security Council auditorium, we were stopped by a young woman who wanted to see our credentials. We only had necklace tags showing that we were with the film team of *End of the Spear*. From her accent, I could tell that the young woman's mother tongue was Spanish.

We began to converse in Spanish as she pressed for more information about the nature of our business in a sensitive part of the United Nations. After I explained about the movie and why we were showing it at the UN, the young floor monitor seemed satisfied that it was okay for us to be looking around in her area. But she wanted to know more about the movie. I wondered if maybe I had been wrong about the kind of people who made up the United Nations staff. As I was soon to discover, there were a lot more staffers like this young lady who wanted to know more about this story of transformation and forgiveness.

When our guide finally led us to the UN theater, quite a few people were milling around in the corridor outside. I was introduced to several diplomats who clearly had no idea who I was.

Maybe these people are here for some other reason than to see the movie, I thought. Then I began to catch pieces of conversations between the people who had invited us to come and other UN functionaries: ". . . but he cannot be turned away; he is a full ambassador and he came specifically to see the movie," I heard someone say.

"But we were personally invited to come, and our delegation

has even arrived early; some provision must be made for us to see this important film," another woman insisted.

"We have already turned away more guests than we can seat in the auditorium. It would be impossible to make special allowances after turning away so many," the person at the door said again and again. Not only was *End of the Spear* going to be shown at the UN, the auditorium was packed and diplomats were being turned away. Most people going to commercial theaters to see the movie already knew something about the story. And normally, when people found out I was an actual character in the movie, it was difficult to get away without at least answering questions and having my picture taken with them. But at the UN, none of the audience seemed to know what or whom the story was about. Yet for some reason they wanted to see it, even if they had to push and shove a bit to get in.

I realized that the diplomats I had met after the January 19 showing really must have talked up the movie to their colleagues. Few people in the audience seemed to know the particulars about the story, but a lot of them showed up and were determined to see it.

I was anxious and a little apprehensive about what this extremely cosmopolitan audience would think of the movie. I have seen *End of the Spear* many times, but every time I watch it with a new group of people, I find myself watching it from their point of view. Christians tend to listen for "Christianese," language that signals that the film is truly a "Christian movie." Just a little too much religious terminology and secular audiences who suspect that *End of the Spear* is a churchy film disconnect from the story.

This United Nations audience was a rainbow of nationalities

and represented a broad spectrum of ages, colors, sizes, and shapes. I had no idea how they would react. I found myself almost holding my breath waiting for some indication of their reaction. When the movie was over, however, I realized that about a quarter of the way through, I had gotten drawn into the story once more and had forgotten to watch for audience reactions.

As soon as the lights came on, our host introduced Jim Hanon, the movie's director, and asked for his comments. He stood up smiled, introduced me, and sat down again. *How does he get away with that?* I wondered, as I tried to think what I could say that would be of interest to this spectacularly diverse audience.

I was nervous. Having grown up overseas, I went to school with children of numerous diplomats. I had learned that what you say and how you say it—especially in a highly charged and sometimes hypersensitive political environment like the one we were in—can be explosive if you are not completely up-to-date on the latest international sensitivities and ideas of political correctness. I was over my head and I knew it.

My hard drive was spinning as I tried to latch onto some thematic thread around which to weave some anecdotes about the making of the film or the story of the film. But when I stepped up on the stage and turned to face the audience, the first person to catch my attention was a woman about a third of the way back on the far right side. I could see that something was wrong with her. At first I thought she was having an asthma attack. Or maybe she was choking on something. I wondered why no one was helping her, and then it dawned on me that what looked like mild convulsions were actually sobs of grief in response to the film. Time seemed to stand still as I let my eyes wander over the rest of the audience. People were openly crying all over the theater.

The diplomat from Central America must have been right. Many of the people in the audience were probably career diplomats. They were spending their lives trying to put out human misery with extinguishers that were not charged, did not work, or were only temporarily effective. These were the professionals who were exposed every day to the worst atrocities that humans perpetrate on their fellow human beings. Their objective—human peace—has proven to be as elusive as perpetual motion. Put out one fire of human greed or hate and another one springs up. Get one hot spot under control and the next thing you know it is a full-blown blaze again.

After I spent a few minutes trying to explain what it was like to love the man who had killed my father, and what it was like to be loved by him, I stepped off the platform, and the showing at the United Nations was over. But the audience did not want to leave. One man from a central African country took me by the arm.

"My story is just like yours," he began, "only profoundly different." That sounded like diplomatic talk for sure. "My father was also speared and hacked to death in the genocides in my country. In that, we are the same. But my father's killer is in prison for life, and I cannot forgive him."

I looked closely at the diplomat. We were both men showing signs of growing old. We had both experienced what the world calls tragedy when the fathers we loved were violently taken from us. Why had my grief turned to joy while his was like shackles weighing him down?

I thought of the saying, "Hurt people hurt people." This man had been hurt, and he wanted those who had hurt him to be hurt in return. That is natural and understandable. But his hatred was not hurting his enemy; it seemed to be killing the diplomat himself instead. I once heard someone say that hatred is suicide on the installment plan. This man seemed to be an example of that proverb.

So what can keep hurt people from hurting people? Maybe it is as simple as this: Forgiven people can forgive people. Lyrics of a song come to mind: "He paid a debt He did not owe; I owed a debt I could not pay. I needed someone to wash my sin away. And now I sing a brand-new song: Amazing Grace. Christ paid the debt that I could never pay."

Contrary to conventional wisdom, you can't alter the fundamental human passions of hedonism, hate, greed, and lust for power by changing human circumstances. Evil comes out of our hearts. To change evil requires us to change our hearts (see Mark 7:21-23). A better economy, a nicer place to work, and more leisure time won't change our base nature.

Give a hateful man a nice place to live, and you'll have a comfortable hater. Give a greedy person a good job with good wages, and that person will want even more. Give power to someone who yearns for it, and you will corrupt him in direct proportion to the amount of power you give him. Give a child who shoplifts a good education, and she will engineer a hostile takeover and steal the entire store.

What we had just seen on the big screen at the union of world nations was a real-life demonstration of the truth that if someone's heart is changed, the most violent and ruthless person can become gentle and kind and dependable. If Mincaye and I, who *should* be enemies, could become family to each other, maybe swords can be beaten into plows, and tanks can be used to pull them. A person's heart is the key. Change someone's heart and you can change the world. Leave that heart unchanged and the world will remain an armed camp.

Later in the day that the movie was shown, we were taken to a reception, where those who had seen the movie could discuss it, meet the people involved, and get more of the story. I was trying to stay out of the way, when the elevator next to the reception area opened. A man who turned out to be a European diplomat saw me and marched straight to me. "I ken note stey," he said with his heavily accented English. "But Ai hed to tel yu dat de movie ve soew hes taken over my mynd. Oal efternoon Ai ken note work, Ai onlee thenk of this story end vonder, *Hou ken such a ting bee?* Now I hev come to tel yu tank yu for showing ous dis film."

It occurred to me that for someone too busy to stay for the reception, he had certainly come out of his way just to say thank you, and I realized he really meant it. *End of the Spear* had been the start of something for him.

Right behind that man, a woman from Argentina arrived. She was in a hurry as well. Her English was as good as my Spanish, so we switched back and forth. *"Yo tambien quiero agradecerte,"* she said—"I also want to thank you." She must have overheard my previous conversation. "I also cannot stay, but I want you to know that I am a career diplomat born to career diplomats. I have lived all over the world. I am a professional.

"I went to see the movie this morning, although I was in a hurry because I had some very important meetings immediately following the screening. But something very strange happened to me. In each of my meetings I began to cry and could not stop. My colleagues were not used to such behavior from me and insisted that I tell them what was wrong. I explained that nothing had personally happened to me. I had just heard a story in a movie, and no doubt it was affecting me. They could not believe that seeing a movie could affect me so deeply. They insisted that I tell them the story. All afternoon, all I have done is tell this story of love and forgiveness. I had to tell you how deeply this story you all have told has affected me and now a number of others I have told."

As the diplomat from Argentina left, the reception room began to fill up. I was introduced to several diplomats from a staunchly communistic country. *They must be atheists,* I thought as I shook their hands. *I don't know how to explain the gospel to atheists.*

Several diplomats from a militant Muslim country arrived next. I knew that there were Christians in that country as well, but that they make up only about half of one percent of the population. *What is the chance that they would send Christians to the UN to represent their country? How do I explain that Jesus claimed He is the Way, the Truth, and the Life, and that no one can come to Allah but by Him?*

As the reception drew to a close, I knew if I wasn't careful, I could start a new Middle East conflict with a few insensitive comments. But then it occurred to me that I would not speak about those issues at all. I would merely tell them some funny Mincaye stories, and then I would tell them what Mincaye would tell them about walking *Waengongi's* trail if he could have been at the reception.

I have been Mincaye's translator long enough that I can usually figure out the theme of what he is going to say even before he speaks. I was pretty sure what Grandfather Mincaye would have wanted to say to this international audience: "Before, no one ever having shown us the Creator's markings, we did not know how to live. Hating and killing, we lived furious and afraid all the time. But then, seeing the Creator's markings, some of us decided to follow the trail He marked with His Son's own blood. That is a very good trail.

"Now, walking *Waengongi's* trail, I live happily and in peace," I said, using a literal translation of what Mincaye says when he talks about the changes in his life from the old way to the new. I went on to explain that Mincaye and the other Waodani who were significant characters in *End of the Spear* had at first said no to the making of the movie. And then I told the small international gathering how I had explained what had happened at Columbine High School so the Waodani would realize that they aren't the only ones who struggle with hatred and the desire for revenge.

When the Waodani heard about North American young people killing each other *ononki*—for no reason—they immediately changed their minds about giving permission for the movie to be made.

"I say, 'Yes!'" Mincaye had exclaimed. "You tell these *cowodi* that I say yes to making a 'veedayo' of our story. Show how we used to live hating and afraid all the time. Then, truly, truly show how those of us who walk *Waengongi's* trail now live happily and in peace. Maybe the foreigners, seeing our people's story, can themselves learn to live happily and in peace too."

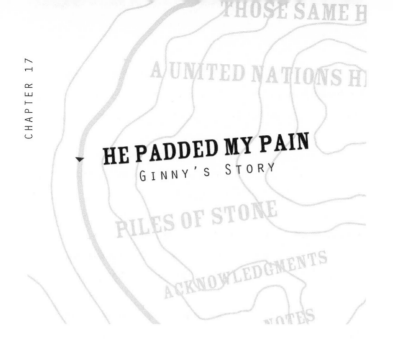

CHAPTER 17

HE PADDED MY PAIN
GINNY'S STORY

I was in my midforties and an empty nester before my time. My chosen career had come to a premature end. All three of our boys had gotten married in the last year and a half. Stephenie, my "Dolly," was traveling around the world with other young people in a Youth for Christ music group. Steve was on the go too, traveling, speaking, and working on other people's problems.

I was used to Steve being gone a fair bit, even though we both yearned to be together more. I had also gotten used to our three boys being gone when they were all away at the University of Florida. But up to this point, I had still had my baby, Steph. Then suddenly she was off in places like India and Trinidad. I got her news by e-mail almost every day—thank God for "pocket e-mailers"—but I couldn't hold her, and I really could not unburden my heart to her online. It just wasn't the same.

With my first three pregnancies, I never asked God for any

divine intervention. He gave us three healthy, happy, make-my-life-busy-and-very-full boys. But by my fourth and what I thought might be my last pregnancy, I prayed for a little girl. I got my wish.

Steve had not wanted any of our boys to have his name. He knew how difficult it was to grow up in his father's huge shadow. In fact, he is still called Nate all the time. I think he kind of enjoys the mistake, but he wanted our boys to have their own identities. When we found out number four was a girl, I wanted to name her after Steve. His eyes lit up when I suggested it, so we named our only daughter Stephenie Raquel Saint.

She became my "Dolly" and to Steve she was the "Dolly Princess." To her three big brothers she was "Mother Superior." It was very special having a little girl after three rambunctious boys. But it was even more special having Steph. She was pretty, feminine, emotional—all girl.

As she grew up, she always had friends, but she did not need to hang out with them all the time. She needed me, and I quickly began to need her—not just as a daughter, but as my friend. In *Anne of Green Gables*, Anne refers to Diana as her bosom friend. Stephenie and I were definitely bosom friends. And we loved watching that movie and other chick flicks together.

When I met Steve, I knew what I wanted to be and what I wanted to do with my life. And I was fortunate to get my wishes in life earlier than most women do. Contentment cuts through a lot of life's complexity, I believe. Some women want a professional career. Some just think they *should* want one. I got a nursing degree, but I love the luxury of being a full-time wife and a mother.

My mother-in-law used to encourage me whenever we'd see the ways in which society looks down on stay-at-home moms: "Ginny, stick to your guns. If God has called you to be a wife and a mother, don't stoop to being a queen."

Once God gave Steve and me our three boys, the only thing I still longed for was a daughter—and one good girlfriend. I was surprised to realize that even when she was just a little girl, Dolly had become that friend. She was extremely capable of expressing herself from a very young age, and she thought about issues far beyond her years. She was mentally sharp, but even more, she was very observant and inquisitive about life. She began to ask me deep questions about moral issues as soon as she started school. These were not subjects of debate in first grade, I knew. Steph just realized that people needed fences to know where they belonged. She understood that the fences don't mean prison walls if we accept them. They protect us from the painful consequences that come from making bad choices when we live without limitations.

All parents think their children are above average, right? I come from Minnesota Scandinavian stock, not far from Garrison Keillor's Lake Wobegon, "where all the children are above average." Taking that into consideration, I think Steph truly did possess a higher level of understanding than most kids. On her SATs, Stephenie earned a score of 730 out of 800 on the math section. On the verbal, she scored a perfect 800. That did not make life easy, but it did tend to keep monotony at bay.

One day as I was waiting in the car lineup at school to pick up the kids, I saw Dolly walking behind two little boys from her class. She was wagging her finger at them, and I could see that her mouth was going a mile a minute. As soon as she hit the seat next to me, she burst into tears. This was not totally unusual. Steph put her all into everything, whether it was having fun, being a pest, or righting the world's wrongs. Today, it was the latter. The two boys she had been lecturing were ringleaders who had just given a substitute teacher a hard time in the last class. Steph was born with a soft place in her heart for the disadvantaged, whether it was a baby squirrel that had fallen out of its nest or a handicapped child who was being teased. She got that from me. But unlike me, she also had Steve's verbal skills and the aggressive nature to do something about injustice. She had let those two boys have it with both barrels.

I knew Stephenie might have had good reason to be upset, but I made the mistake of suggesting that maybe she should let the school faculty correct the problem. Steph could not do that. She could not just stand by and let people be hurt, especially people who could not defend themselves. Steph could not and would not hide her feelings. Everyone knew that if you picked on little guys, down-and-outers, or the defenseless around Dolly, you did it at your own peril. But few saw her very tender heart like I did. Even when she took the bullies to task, her heart broke for them, too. She knew that sooner or later they would end up lonely and ostracized because they had not learned to control themselves.

I marveled that such a small child could understand concepts that I had not picked up until much later in life. It seemed as if Steph were trying to cram a lifetime into the first few chapters of her story.

Another day, we made it to the house before the tears exploded.

"What is wrong this time?" I asked Steph. Her cries turned

to sobs, and she poured out her heart to me. She was in about fifth grade by this time.

"Oh, Mom, I have so many answers . . . and no one is asking me the questions."

As she grew older, one of Steph's greatest frustrations was that friends who claimed to be Christians could be so inconsistent. Boys would pray in public at the Christian school and then make nasty sexual comments about girls once they were outside. She called her girlfriends to task for asking God to protect them and then wearing what she considered to be provocative clothes. She did not think that was fair for either God or the boys.

I watched my little girl wrestle with life, and I tried to explain what I had learned from my many more years of experience. But even I did not understand how perceptive this little girl who had been entrusted to me was.

Steph had always loved children and babies. One day, early in the morning, she came to me, and I could tell that something was troubling her.

"Mom," she told me, "I just dreamed you were pregnant. I was so excited I couldn't wait to tell everyone. Then I woke up." She hoped against hope that I really was pregnant with a baby for her to care for. I hated to have to tell Dolly that I wasn't pregnant. We would not have a new baby until she was in high school and we had moved down to live with Steve's jungle family.

One Waodani woman in particular really took to me and Steph, whom they called *Nemo*—Star. Marga's mother was Waodani, but her father had been one of the last full-blooded men from the Zaparo tribe. Marga wasn't completely accepted by the other Waodani, so she understood how difficult it was for me to take care of my family in this very different world. Marga took it upon herself to help me with the wild pig meat that was frequently given to me—bristles, coagulated blood, and all—or the giant slabs of delicious catfish with half the whiskered heads still attached. She would take my game down to the river to wash and butcher it. She taught Steph how to make string, weave net bags, make plantain drink, and work the garden.

She also decided that we needed a baby. She would take care of that for us too. Marga was like a baby factory. At about thirty, she got pregnant with her eighth child while we lived in the hut next to hers. When her beautiful baby girl was born in the predawn hours one damp morning, she cut the umbilical cord and sent the precious bundle up to our house with her oldest daughter, Nemonta. She made it clear that although the baby was biologically hers, she wanted us to raise and care for her. Stephenie and I were overjoyed, and we named this precious baby Ana Beth. We loved our little olive-skinned baby, and we loved Marga for wanting to be tied to us for life.

Stephenie and I grew even closer as she rapidly matured living in the jungles for a year and a half. As her long, slender body began to develop the curves of womanhood, she sometimes pointed out her physical flaws to me.

"Your pop loves me so much I don't think he even sees my physical flaws," I said. "We'll find you a husband who will feel the same way about you."

"Yeah, Mom, but Pop overlooks your physical deficiencies because you are so sweet," she said. "My husband is going to need a great body."

Stephenie was sixteen when we returned to the States; tall

and beautiful, with long blond hair, she began to attract the attention of boys right away. She noticed them too, but she agreed with her pop that dating was more like trial divorce. Then she found herself interested in a heartthrob from Jesse's class. He must have been interested too. At the very end of his senior year, this young man asked Stephenie out on a date. She really liked him, but she turned him down. He had been voted "heartbreaker of the class," and although she was a normal girl with normal interests, Steph hated the pain of rejection that seemed to be an integral part of the dating scene. She had decided that her dad was probably right; there had to be a better way of finding a life partner than dating.

"Mr. Popular" came back a couple of days later and told Steph that she *had* to go out with him. "So I can get my pride back," he said.

"I give you your pride back," Stephenie answered, "but I still won't go out with you."

This young lady who was my daughter was absolutely unmovable when she believed principle was at stake. I found myself admiring and looking up to my own daughter.

I had barely gotten used to living back in the States with my refrigerator, stove, dishwasher, and car again when it was time for Steph to go to college. She didn't go far. She gave a thought or two to studying medicine, but she did not want that kind of a career. She wanted to have at least ten children, and she wanted to homeschool them all. So she decided to get a degree in something she loved: piano.

I had started taking Dolly to piano lessons when she was six. I always looked forward to Stephenie's weekly piano lessons. We had a half hour each way to ourselves, and we often shared our hopes and aspirations for life with each other. We also discussed our weaknesses and fears. We were mother and daughter, but Steph was a wise little woman who understood me in a way that no one else ever could. I loved those special times with my little girl.

By the time Steph was in ninth grade, her piano teacher asked her to teach the younger children. Steph really enjoyed that. She decided that was what she wanted to do with her life. Like her piano teacher, she wanted to have a conservatory at home so she could help with financial support while still taking care of the family she dreamed of having.

In the summer after Stephenie's first year at the University of Florida, we visited family in Minnesota. We went to a concert put on by a Youth for Christ musical group. After the concert I bumped into the director, a man I had gone to school with. He mentioned that they were desperately looking for a pianist to travel with the group the next year. Steve said that Stephenie was a wonderful pianist, but as he said it, a look almost like fear crossed his face. I wasn't sure what Steve's look meant, but I was excited about what could be a great experience for our Dolly. Now I realize that Steve must have known that our little girl's life was about to change. He was not ready to be separated from his only little girl. I wasn't either, but somehow I wasn't worried.

I should have been. I had no idea how profoundly Stephenie's absence would affect me. Often, while she was gone, I yearned to hold her; I ached to unburden my heart to the person who understood me better than any other person alive. I found myself lonely, and I missed the way that Stephenie had needed me. I longed for the day she would come home. And then, at long last, that day arrived. We picked Stephenie up at the airport in Orlando. Steve waited with Steph for the baggage to come out while I watched from the car and soaked her in visually. She was five-foot-nine-inches tall and thin in a curvaceous and feminine way, dressed in jeans with black boots and a black leather jacket over an embroidered white sleeveless cotton blouse. Her long blond hair was pulled in front of her right shoulder, and she was leaning on Steve. As they drank each other in, my heart melted with a sense of goodness and relief.

I don't remember much about the ride home. My heart was overflowing, and life was good. I was complete again. We also had two new babies in the family, our first grandchildren. Steph was overjoyed at the prospect that she and I would be part of raising these first two babies of the new generation. I knew there would be some tears when Stephenie realized that her sisters-in-law would want to be involved too.

When we got home from the airport, we had a welcome-home party for Stephenie. I realized I needed some last-minute things from the store and was just about to take off when Steph stopped me. I explained that I was just going to run to the store and would be right back. She was tired, and I wanted her to relax.

"Momma, I can't just let you go by yourself," she told me. So off we went, just the two of us. Words can't express how profoundly grateful I am now that my little girl did not want me to go to the store alone that day. I had no way of knowing it, but that was the last time I would ever get to spend alone with my "little" girl.

By the time we got back from the store, it was about nine o'clock at night. Steph had the beginnings of a headache and said she wanted to rest a bit. What we didn't know at the time was that her headache was being caused by a cerebral aneurysm.

Stephenie asked me to go back to her room with her, and then she asked me to call "Pop." She wanted us to pray for her. I sat on the bed holding this precious gift God had given to us as Steve prayed that He would take her headache away. The blood vessel broke, and my precious daughter slipped into a coma in my arms.

Steve has told and written about the details of the agonizing hours that followed. What I remember most vividly and carry in my heart with clearest recollection is the mercy God showed me during that terrible agony.

I sat by Steph's bed in intensive care and held the slender hand that was so familiar to me. I felt the slight bulge on her left wrist where she had fallen and broken it in our backyard. I felt the little dimple on her lower right side—she called it "Smiley"—it reminded me of the ruptured appendix that had almost taken her life. Steve had been on a trip to Thailand during that emergency, and I had learned to really trust God during those frightening days. I remembered the verse God had given me during that surgery: "Don't worry about anything; instead, pray about everything" (Philippians 4:6).

I rubbed Stephenie's feet and those long toes that were so elegantly different from my own short ones. As she lay in a coma, I remembered how easily she had adapted to life in the jungle. She wouldn't even wear boots most of the time. She had gone barefoot so much that her toes had begun to spread like those of the Waodani's.

In anticipation of her death, the doctors asked us to make some very difficult decisions. A transplant team wanted permission to harvest Stephenie's organs so that other people could live. They wanted to take pieces of my Dolly and sew her into strange bodies. I couldn't say no, but I prayed, *Oh God, please not her heart. Please make them leave her sensitive heart alone. I can't let them have her heart.*

I felt so selfish, but I just couldn't bear to think about someone taking Stephenie's heart.

Later, we received letters from a number of appreciative transplant recipients who received Steph's two kidneys, her liver, and her pancreas. Steve called to ask the transplant team about her heart. As it turns out, they did not transplant Steph's heart. By the time they were ready to take it, her body had shut down too far. Once again, God proved His love to me in my most difficult hour.

Our boys and their wives and our two new granddaughters gathered at our house as Steve and I waited at the hospital for the end. By then, it was clear that only divine intervention in the form of a resurrection miracle could bring Steph back to us. Our precious little girl had already been pronounced clinically dead. A reporter named Marian came by our house to ask for some personal information to include in Stephenie's obituary. As I was answering her questions, she asked, "Did Stephenie by any chance go to the Christian school down the street?"

When I said she had, Marian got excited and told me, "I know Steph."

She went on to tell me about how she used to substitute teach at that school, and that one particular day she was having a terrible time controlling a classroom full of kids. Suddenly a young girl stood up and admonished the students who were disrupting class. "That was such an unusual thing for a young person to do—standing up for a substitute teacher. I remembered her name. It was Stephenie. That was your little girl, wasn't it?"

"Yes, that *was* my little girl." After the reporter left, I wandered through the house looking at our precious sons, their sweet wives, and our two darling grandchildren asleep on the couches and floor of our family room. I was overwhelmed with a very peculiar feeling of wonder: first, that God had given us such a happy home, and then that He had entrusted Stephenie Raquel to my care for twenty years and twenty days. My heart should have been in pain and agony, but instead, an inexpressible sense of peace and well-being flooded through me.

If Stephenie had died a week earlier, she would have been in Trinidad. We probably would not have even been able to get there to help bury her beautiful body. A day earlier, and she would have been in Minnesota. One week later, and Steve would have been at a conference in Amsterdam, and Steph and I would have been on our way to Alabama to visit Shaun and Anne.

Shortly after she died, I had a dream about Steph. She was sitting on the foot of our bed, and she was beautiful and radiant. But something was different. I realized what it was just before I woke up. She was as beautiful and full of life as ever, but the pain and concerns of life were gone. I could still feel the dream after I was fully awake, and I reveled in its luxury. I was sure that my little girl was still alive, but the concerns and disappointments of this life were all behind her.

I was standing on our back step recently, thinking about Stephenie. I knew I would miss her terribly, but I had no idea how deep the pain would go and how long it would last. Sometimes it is like a searing burn deep in my being. But I would never ask for her back. As I thought about this, I felt God tell me, *Oh Ginny, I'm so sorry that I had to take your Dolly. But I made it as easy as I could.*

Oh, thank you, God, for bringing her home to take her home.

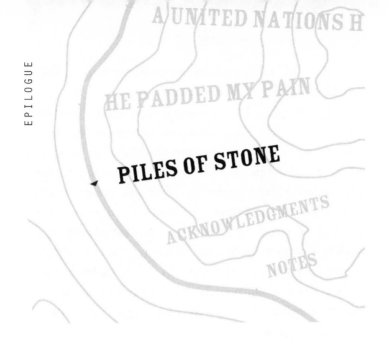

PILES OF STONE

+

I had been tense for three days. Three days of life hanging in the balance. Three sleepless nights.

I glanced at my watch—5:00 a.m. It was still dark. If the killer was going to show up, it was as likely now as later, after the sun came up. We had been told to wait for seventy-two hours. But I figured sixty-five hours was close enough.

+

Not wanting to wake up Ginny—she had been terrorized enough by the events of the last week and especially these last three days—I slipped quietly out of bed and into the dark hallway.

The first door on the left was ajar. Slowly, to make sure there would be no noise, I swung it open just far enough to slip into the room. The only sound was the slight whisper of the door rubbing the top of the carpet.

Was the intruder here in Jaime Nate's room? By the faint light of a streetlamp half a block away, I could see Jaime in his bed. There was no movement. I tried to detect a sign of breathing—nothing. My heart almost stopped.

I knew that these last three days had been real, even though they didn't feel real. They weren't just a dream, as I had hoped. No amount of hoping or praying would change the state of affairs now. But wait a minute. If God is God, and if He cares, why couldn't He change the lump from one arm to the other? Why couldn't He just make the disease—or whatever it was— go away? He could if He wanted to. *Oh, God, please let this be nothing. Please, please, oh please. Let it be me, if need be, but please not fun-loving, happy little Jaime Nate. Oh, please let this pass.*

I was past worrying now about waking Jaime Nate or anyone else in the house. The huge, all-consuming question was this: Was our son going to live or die?

Jaime's right arm was hanging limply over the side of the bed. I lifted it gently and rubbed my fingers down his forearm. It wasn't there. It had to be the other arm. I lifted his right arm, and there was the bump. I rubbed my finger over it two more times. There was no mistaking it. There was a significant welt on his right forearm. This would spell the difference between devastating reality and wonderful relief.

But suddenly I realized that I could not remember which arm was which.

Jaime had complained of his arm being sore a week ago, and Ginny had found a lump in his armpit. We didn't think it was serious, but we were still mildly concerned, so we took him in to see our family doctor. Our concern quickly moved from mild to gut wrenching. After some tests, our doctor told us matter-of-factly, "This looks like it might be lymphoma." *Cancer! Cancer?* One word and our minds began to run wild with dread. Jaime was still just a little boy!

"Do you by any chance have a cat?" the doctor continued. What a question to ask after just breaking the news that our life-loving ten-year-old son might have cancer.

"Yes, we do have a cat. But what does that have to do with lymphoma?" My exasperation at the doctor's insensitivity must have shown.

"Well, this has the telltale symptoms of lymphoma, but there is another possibility that is frequently mistaken for this cancer: cat scratch fever."

After injecting a drop of two different serums under the skin, one on each of Jaime's forearms, the doctor informed us that in three days, one or the other would form a red lump under the skin. Right arm, lymphoma. Left arm, cat scratch fever. Or was it the other way around?

"Ginny, wake up! Ginny, was cat scratch fever the right arm or the left arm?"

She sat up with a start. "I think it was left arm."

"There is a lump on his right arm."

We ran into the kitchen and pulled out the file with the informational brochures the doctor had given us.

Oh, God, please let it be the cat.

"It's the left arm; it is the *left* one." Ginny was shaking.

"What is the left arm?" I was desperate. "Is the left one cancer or cat scratch?" Oh, this was awful. We knew where the lump was—why had I not written *cancer* on one arm and *cat* on the other?

"The left arm is lymphoma."

We both grabbed for Jaime's left arm. There was no lump.

It was over. The sky was just getting light. But it was going to be a bright, sunny, wonderful day.

Now, what do I have going today? I thought. *I'd better get busy. I've already wasted a good bit of the last three days.*

As I drove down the street later that morning, a quote that a good friend of mine uses from time to time came to mind: "Gratitude is the shortest-lived human emotion."

It was true. One minute I was begging God for a miracle, my mind totally consumed with the fate of my son. Fifteen minutes later I was completely preoccupied with inconsequential tasks that I would not even be able to recall in a few days.

Today Jaime is almost thirty. He has three darling little girls. He has had a few colds and the flu once or twice, but at six-foot-three and two hundred pounds, he is tall and handsome and still loves life.

I felt like a worm. One minute I was begging the Creator of the universe for His intervention in my son's life. A few minutes later I was almost embarrassed that I had let my anxiety show. Then it occurred to me: For all I know, God might have changed the lump. Maybe this was a miracle. How could I be so casual?

I went to the other extreme. I wanted to build a monument to God's miraculous intervention in the life of my family.

I wonder what kind of a permit it will require to build and install a monument in the cul-de-sac in front of our house.

I pictured a statue of God holding a ten-year-old boy with a cat curled up at His feet. I was just dreaming. But maybe I *could* build a monument.

There is a historical record of the Egyptian nation enslaving a much smaller group of nomadic people long ago. When the slaves could no longer bear up under the suffering, they called on their God to deliver them. He did.

He sent them a deliverer whom their descendants still revere:

Moses. Then when Pharaoh wouldn't release the slave nation, God sent plagues on the Egyptians. Finally, Pharaoh changed his mind under God's persistent punishment. The Egyptians even gave the Israelites gold and silver, allowing their former slaves to loot them.

God wasn't finished. When the Egyptians changed their minds and sent the army after the fleeing former slaves, God parted the Red Sea and then drowned the Egyptian army. The Israelites had to have been eternally grateful, right? Nope. They complained because they didn't have water. God gave them that. They complained that they didn't have bread. God gave them manna. They griped that they didn't have meat. God provided that. Then they started back in grumping about not having water again at Sinai. Then it was the Amalekites. They were sure they were going to be killed.

When Moses was replaced by Joshua, God came up with a remedy for the constant bickering and complaining. God was going to part the waters of the Jordan River so the Israelites could enter the land He had promised to them. But this time, God wanted these ungrateful people to remember what He had done for them. God told Joshua to pick one man from each of the twelve tribes of Israel. Each man was supposed to pick up a rock from the middle of the Jordan River to be used in building a stone monument—a reminder of what God had just done for them.

Joshua told the people that this would be a reminder not only to them but also to their children after them (see Joshua 4:1-7). This was a tradition for the entire community (see Exodus 20:24). When God intervened in a remarkable way in the lives of the Israelites and reminded them of who He was, they were to build altars of stones as memorials to God's intervention on their behalf.

The children learned that these "piles of stone" represented stories of deliverance.

"Hey, Pop, what's with that pile of stones over there?" a boy might ask his father. "Oh, yeah," would come the reply. "That was a good one. Tell you what, I'll call Mom. We'll order pizza tonight and I'll tell you that story."

I'd guess there was a lot less grumping and complaining after that. Those piles of stone made a difference. Gratitude not only began to last a little longer, it actually began to pass from generation to generation. Don't you sometimes wish you had reminders of the good things you've seen God do as you've walked His trail? Those good things that should not be forgotten—things that are just too good, too unlikely to attribute to luck? I do.

There aren't many rocks in Florida or the Amazon jungles, so I decided that I would build my piles of stone in a written record of all I have seen God do as I've walked His trail. I have passed those stories on to our four children. Now I'm passing them on to our grandchildren. It not only builds a sense of gratitude; it also builds a sense of identity and belonging.

I've only been in Israel one time. I was amazed at how secular that society is. But I was also surprised that the country shut down for a religious holiday while Ginny and I were there. Everyone seemed to be out in the streets celebrating Purim. People exchanged gifts and painted clown faces with huge smiles on themselves. They were celebrating their ancestors' deliverance in the Persian Empire when Esther, a Jewish maiden, was queen. God put her in a position to save her people from destruction.

The people celebrating weren't necessarily people of faith. But still, they celebrated what God had done for them. Holidays such as Yom Kippur, Passover, and Purim not only remind them to be grateful but also give Jews a powerful sense of identity.

We celebrate national holidays that represent great events in our country as well, like the Fourth of July. But what about personal and family memorials to remind us of those special events when we saw God show up along the trail? We need to remember what the Almighty has done for us individually, too. And we need to pass on that knowledge to our children to give them a sense of identity, to teach them gratitude at an early age. We need to let them know that God is going to give them reason to build their own piles of stone.

If you enjoyed these few piles of stone, good. If they bring your own stone pile events to mind, great! And if these stories push you to grab a recorder or a notebook to record your own "God cares and intervened for me" events for your family, friends, and heirs—*perfect*! That is what I hoped to accomplish with this book.

ACKNOWLEDGMENTS

✝

Tyndale team, thanks. You keep reminding Ginny and me that you care. We love the presents you keep sending, but you show us best with the dependable, cheerful help you give with each book. And thanks for giving us Lisa Jackson to shorten and polish what we write.

NOTES

✝

[1] You can read Steve Davis's version of these events in the article "Out of the Sky," published in *The Best Stories from Guideposts* (Carol Stream, IL: Tyndale House Publishers, 1987).

[2] Olive Fleming Liefeld, *Unfolding Destinies: The Ongoing Story of the Auca Mission* (Grand Rapids, MI: Discovery House Publishers, 1998).

[3] Ibid., 48.

[4] Ibid., 55.

[5] Ibid., 155.

[6] Ibid., 182–3.

[7] C. S. Lewis, *The Lion, the Witch and the Wardrobe* (New York: Harper Collins, 1950), 163.

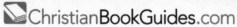

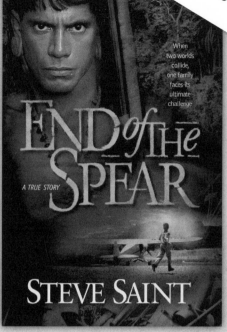

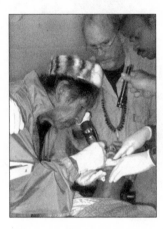

In January of 1956, five men entered the jungle in Ecuador to make contact with a savage tribe . . . and never returned.

Through Gates of Splendor, the best-selling missionary story of the twentieth century, was written in 1956 by Jim Elliot's wife, Elisabeth. Decades later, this story of unconditional love and complete obedience to God still inspires new readers.

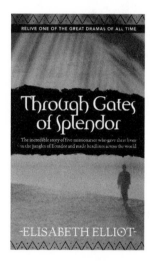

Mass Paperback

50th Anniversary Edition

Also from Tyndale House Publishers

An international best seller!
Experience the thrilling story of missionaries Gracia and Martin
Burnham and their horrific year as hostages of the Abu Sayaaf
terrorist group.

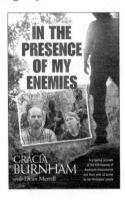 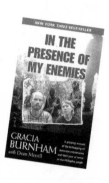

Available in hardcover and Living Book editions

Gracia Burnham reflects on her year of captivity in the
Philippine jungle and the amazing lessons she learned about
God's grace and constant care.

Available in hardcover
and softcover editions

"To know the street children is to have one's life transformed."

When Dr. Chi Huang took a year off from Harvard Medical School to work with orphans and street children in La Paz, Bolivia, he had no idea it would take only that one year to change his life forever.

Through his own story and the stories of Gabriel, Mercedes, Vicki, Daniela, and beautiful little Rosa, "Dr. Chi" gives us a glimpse into the shocking world of children who, betrayed by those who were supposed to protect them, are left to the dangerous freedom of the streets. And he gives us a fleeting glance into his own inner world, where he is forced to confront his past and reexamine his future.

When Invisible Children Sing is an amazing story of faith—faith ignited, challenged, almost abandoned, and ultimately restored. Journey with a remarkable man through a remarkable year and allow your own faith to be ignited, challenged, and renewed.